THE INNOCENCE OF THE EYE
a filmmaker's guide

THE INNOCENCE OF THE EYE
a filmmaker's guide   ed spiegel

SILMAN-JAMES PRESS   LOS ANGELES

First Edition

10 9 8 7 6 5 4 3 2 1

Library of Congress Cataloging-in-Publication Data

Spiegel, Ed. (Edward), 1922–
    The innocence of the eye : a filmmaker's guide / Ed. Spiegel.— 1st ed.
        p. cm.
    ISBN 1-879505-63-0 (alk. paper)
        1. Motion pictures—Production and direction. 2. Motion pictures. 3. Cinematography.
I. Title.

PN1995.9.P7 S667 2002

791.43'023—dc21   2002030581

Printed in the United States of America

SILMAN-JAMES PRESS
1181 Angelo Drive
Beverly Hills, CA 90210

Dedicated to the memory of Slavko Vorkapich:
film director, scholar, painter, teacher, mentor, and friend.

Contents

Contents

Some Preliminaries

An Introduction

In 1946, a remarkable social advance, the GI Bill, paid for my enrollment in the Department of Cinema at the University of Southern California. I held the naively optimistic belief that an education in movies might ensure me an eager welcome at the film studios. The facts, however, proved otherwise. The studios at that time had little or no experience with people formally educated in motion pictures. In that era, USC was virtually the only school offering a degree in the subject. (At the present time, close to a thousand schools of higher learning offer either film courses or a degree at the present time.)

The university itself seemed to have some doubts about the presence of a motion picture department within its halls of academe. True, the cinema department's emphasis at that time was basically technical, largely of the "nuts and bolts" kind—getting cameras in focus and picture and sound track in an intelligible relationship and trying not to burn one's fingers when changing the bulb in a studio light. Merely getting our film efforts developed in the student-run black-and-white 16mm lab was a triumph. If our film returned unmangled from the primitive lab, its images were a disheartening dismal gray. The crisp black-and-white images of Hollywood's product seemed unattainable, denied to presumptuous students by the imperious gods who also guarded studio gates.

Film students in those days had to be content that their cameras recorded an image—any image! Small wonder a self-respecting institution of higher learning had some difficulty acknowledging what might have been viewed as a trade school in its cloistered halls.

The USC movie department was housed—or banished—to an old wooden building on the edge of the main campus near downtown Los Angeles. Rumor had it that the structure had once been stables. Though I never detected an odor, some claimed that the smell of manure still lingered. The building's style was a lowly rustic clapboard rather than the campus's prevailing manicured brick. It was many years later before any advanced degree was offered and years more before graduate students were allowed to prove that making a motion picture might actually demonstrate competence enough for a Masters or a Ph.D. degree. Only a thesis written in dry, analytic, academic style was allowed—in effect, the written word rather than actual filmmaking was the only guarantee of certification.

Today, all this has changed. At USC, the largess of such highly successful graduates as George Lucas and others has helped the department expand and modernize. Film department applicants come endowed with the highest SAT scores of any student group, and for every SAT whiz-kid accepted, ten are turned away. Hollywood agents keep tabs on the brightest who emerge during their schooling, and USC's motion picture and television graduates have achieved a remarkable array of critical distinctions and box-office successes. The motion picture department is no longer a stepchild, but a source of considerable prestige to the university.

The issue of whether a formal education in filmmaking is relevant in the professional world has been answered resolutely in the affirmative.

Slavko Vorkapich

The quality of my education at USC took a sharp turn for the better when a remarkable teacher, Serbian-born Slavko Vorkapich, became head of the film department. Vorkapich occupied a unique niche in the Hollywood scene in the thirties and forties. His specialty was *the film within the film* called the *montage*—the quick juxtaposition of discrete images that, taken together, form a symbol for a larger concept—as well as other strikingly visual, larger production segments. Submerged within the body of larger films, his work was not given much note by the general public, but his peers within the movie industry recognized his brilliant moviemaking. He drew great respect as well for managing an almost totally independent domain within studio walls, uniquely responsible, from conception to execution, for his original creations. To this day, many of his film pieces stand on their own and are often judged as superior to the larger films of which they were a part.

Though Vorkapich had studied painting in Europe, he had felt constrained by his classical academic training. "I was haunted by that old man Michelangelo," he confided to a group of us. Pursuing what was for him a less inhibited mode of expression, he turned to still photography, but it was not until he discovered the power of moving images that he broke free of his archetypal "old man" of the Renaissance. With Robert Florey, he made *The Hollywood Extra*, a stylistic film satire. Costing pennies, filmed largely on a table top, it opened up studio gates and a new career. Vorkapich met a studio need to display what could be a film's costliest big "production" sequences in ways that were exciting but cost relatively little.

The montage form he created was a visual condensation of time. Images in movement were symbols of larger themes: Banners and crossed swords became a substitute for whole armies, the flight of doves expressed the ecstasy of love, grinning skulls were exultant Death.

As he evolved as a film artist, he came to a realization that his symbolic images were often intellectual constructs that were not as emotionally direct as what they represented. When he came to the university to teach, he was conscious that his montage imagery should be experienced in a more profound way and not merely felt kinesthetically or understood intellectually. A motion picture, he confirmed, had to express itself with an imagery rooted in the unconscious mind. What he knew from the start, as well, was that film was like dance—and like the choreographer, the filmmaker should be aware that movement, besides creating a visceral response, was itself emotional and symbolic.

Vorkapich stood to one side of the Hollywood mainstream. Beside his film executions, he was developing an unorthodox but convincing and consistent theory of film art. This was the basis for his desire to teach.

Motion and the Written Language

Ascending motion, Vorkapich pointed out, suited the sense of liberation, of hope, a rising toward heaven. Descending motion—in a proper context—could express an ending, a surrender, or dying.

Motion is a metaphor that is the formative kernel of many verbal phrases. The motion incorporated in verbal expression attests to movement's significance as symbol.

Movement as metaphor

Ascending as a positive: uplifted, on the way up, reaching for the sky, the rising spirit, soaring (in the sense of liberation), climbing upward, picking yourself up, things looking up, climbing to the top, top-flight, reaching the pinnacle of success, heightened, free as a bird, etc.

Descending as a negative: down in the dumps, it's a downer, underfoot, getting in deeper, downward spiral, going to hell, down on one's knees, hitting ground zero or bottom, falling short, plumbing the depths, flattened, squashed, crushed, pulverized, depressed, digging oneself into a hole, etc.

Other metaphors from motion: spinning out of control, swallowed up, hand-cuffed, crippled, groping (in the sense of seeking understanding), rocking the boat, peppered, showered, rattled, hammered, muddied, clobbered, battered, burnt out, giving up, twisted, spinning, liquidating, etc.

Motion as Dramatic Statement

Early in my career, I did some second-unit direction for which I had to shoot a simple scene in which two men stand next to their car parked at the edge of a cliff and look down. They see that events have turned against them. One actor had a single line recognizing defeat: "I'll have to tell New York about this."

It was a very minor piece of the whole film, and it would probably have sufficed to have the actor say the line, get into his car, and go. Perhaps because this was my very first chance at directing a professional actor, I wanted to do as much as I could with my little opportunity. I decided that the act of sitting down into the car could also be a metaphor for defeat, so I asked the actor to seem to collapse into the car seat and then say his line followed by slamming the door shut as if he were closing himself off from all hope of getting his way. A minor bit of business, but I felt I had utilized all the visual elements within the scene to heighten the moment of drama.

This little experience taught me something valuable. Every filmmaking experience, no matter how slight, should be considered as an opportunity to expand one's understanding of the craft. This is not as obvious as it may seem. It requires making the effort to understand what cinematic principles may underlie something that works for you on the screen.

The Innocence of the Eye

A dance, whether executed by a physically present human being or by motion picture images, is first experienced on a primitive level that precedes intellectual cognition. Vorkapich borrowed a phrase from gestalt psychology, "the innocence of the eye," to describe this primitive response. It was an integral part of his theory of film. I consider his view a theory of filmic dance, a form not dependent on literary or dramatic antecedents.

He hoped that his views would provoke the evolution of a motion picture art separate from what he pointedly called "the photoplay." He longed to see the medium develop out of its essential characteristics, which he saw—not surprisingly—as motion and picture.

The arrival of Vorkapich at USC's film department created an enormous stir. The student body and faculty divided ardently into pro and con Vorkapich camps, defenders of the photoplay versus motion imagery enthusiasts. Vorkapich enjoyed the controversy he caused and saw the ferment as creative. Though he relished debate and the open discussion of conflicting opinion, he could not bear the subtler, more devious antagonisms and maneuvers arising out of political turf battles and jealousy. Vorkapich challenged assumptions upon which some of the faculty had based entire careers. This group had influence with the university administrators. Eventually Vorkapich began to feel that his teaching was being sabotaged. Among his pet expressions was one I both admired and rued. "I've always got my hat in my hand," he'd tell us, meaning that when he was not allowed to achieve his artistic goals, he was ready to walk away. I felt he resigned his position at USC too readily after only a year and a half on the job.

His impact on many of the students had by then already been considerable. Among them was Conrad Hall, who would become one of the film industry's most renowned cinematographers. This two-time Academy Award winner and nine-time award nominee considered his encounter with Vorkapich "life changing," largely for the very reason of Slavko's adherence, above all, to an uncompromising artistic standard. When Vorkapich resigned from USC, but saw himself continuing in a role as a teacher of film theory, Conrad, among quite a few other students, followed him to his home in Benedict Canyon, where he continued his classes.

Conrad told me recently that he had been inspired by Vorkapich's ability "to engender the spirit in us that we were developing a new language, that movies weren't just about drama, but learning how to use the tools to *create* drama."

Vorkapich devoted himself to further refining his ideas and their presentation via film demonstrations. He designed a series of ten lectures that he was invited to deliver at New York's Museum of Modern Art. These lectures, covered enthusiastically in film journals, grew into a major event in New York's film world. Their effect rippled out into the broader film community. Vorkapich was hired by a large commercials house to lecture its directors and producers. Nationally, he was invited to give his lecture series at major universities, including Harvard, UCLA, and, perhaps not surprisingly, back at USC.

The effect of his teaching was to influence the USC motion picture department for many years, just as his examples and concepts have permeated the professional world of movies and television. These effects are most recognizable in the visual brilliance of many television commercials and in the choreography that is in the design of numerous action scenes within feature films. His philosophy of film aesthetics comes into play wherever a synthesis of evocative images and motion are used to enhance the viewer's experience.

Before he departed USC, Vorkapich made a prescient statement that the years and my own career have confirmed as true many times over. He said students didn't have to embrace his whole dream of a future motion picture form "free from the shackles of the photoplay" to gain an advantage from his teaching. His "cinematic principles," he said, "*can make any kind of film better.*"

That statement is the inspiration for *The Innocence of the Eye*. The cinematic principles described in this book are the bedrock that enhanced my career and to which I have added insights gained from my own fifty years of moviemaking experience.

Learning the Craft

Despite the advantages an education in moviemaking can offer, what skills most successful moviemakers acquire are learned largely from seeing lots of movies. In our contemporary culture, even without adding pedagogical analysis, sights and sounds from movie and television screens come in a near continuous bombardment. Moviemaking seemingly could be absorbed as readily as the spoken language. However, it is not quite that simple. All art forms are a seduction, an experience perpetrated in disguise. The untrained eye rarely sees the manner of painting beneath the perceived landscape on a canvas, the untrained ear is rarely aware of the principles that guide the structure of a symphony.

Learning moviemaking by absorption works better for some than others. It relies more on unconsciously acquired material and intuition than on rational analysis. It is typically a piecemeal process without a view to general principles. Why something "works" brilliantly on one occasion but fails in the filmmaker's next project can remain a mystery to the intuitive filmmaker. Vorkapich contended that such unpredictable performance can often be attributed to a failure to understand underlying cinematic principles—understood intuitively in one instance, but not forthcoming in another. A rational understanding of basic principles might clarify that insight.

These principles amount to a theory of motion pictures. An understanding of this theory, then, is the first step in understanding the craft.

A danger in this theoretical approach to a motion picture education should be admitted at the start. Theory cannot describe a movie experience any better than a description of a symphony can approximate hearing the music. Theorizing has its limitations. Whatever theory one studies must, in the final sense, be translated into something *felt* because of what happens on the screen. Vorkapich often quoted the German writer Goethe, who reminded us that "gefuhl ist alles"—feeling is all! All true filmmakers are also guided by the expression "the screen will tell." No script, no good intentions, no director's or producer's or actor's track record of success can deny that *ultimate* truth. The only proof of a film's effectiveness is what's on the screen. This book, among other things, aims to alert the reader to what to look for and what to plan for as a means of evoking emotion by motion picture (filmic) techniques.

Documentary, Stage, and Drama: A History

Before the potential of film or its limitations can be understood, one should at least pay attention briefly to the way that it has evolved.

Documentation—putting scenes on film to make a record—was undoubtedly the first use for motion pictures. In the earliest days of this new technology, an audience was satisfied simply to see things move. A shot of a steam locomotive fast approaching the camera thrilled viewers, some of whom reportedly ducked down to escape the onrushing phantom image.

The camera reached out and recorded motion scenes from all over the world, clearly proving superior in many aspects to an album of still pictures. But cameras were not particularly mobile, and travelogues of town squares, scenic vistas, and even unclothed native peoples grew tiresome. It then followed that arranged scenes were brought to play in front of the cameras. Films began to be designed to tell stories. French pioneer Georges Méliès fashioned short films, such as *A Trip to the Moon*, for which he fantasized an entirely original world within the screen's window. Filming stage plays was an obvious direction to pursue. Adding visual titles for dialogue somewhat compensated for the absence of sound, but the attraction of the actor's living presence was only hinted at in this new two-dimensional, black-and-white image of reality etched on silver-halide film emulsion and projected onto a flat screen. It soon became apparent that recording a single camera's point of view of a stage play failed to convey the excitement and vitality of the original play. Absent was the actor's living presence and three-dimensional reality. Also lacking was the live stage play's tension of unpredictability and the shared "vibes" between performer and audience that fed a sense of engagement with the play's events.

In a very early film short called *The Life of the Fireman*, the revolutionary discovery was made that cutting to a closeup, which in effect separated the actor's head from the rest of his body, was not, as some had thought, disturbing to an audience and did not suggest that some mayhem had occurred. In the effort to add life to the photographed stage play, closeup angles allowed the actor to communicate more easily and with a greater range of meaning. His enlarged face shown on a lighted screen in a darkened theater could transfix an audience with an almost hypnotic intensity. There followed the additional discovery that it was not necessary to maintain the single point of view of the theater. The camera could present continuous action from multiple points of view, which began the serious evolution of the photoplay format—giving an audience a range of visual experience it had never gotten from the live stage. These developments compensated in large measure for the loss of the actor's actual presence.

With multiple points of view came an expansion of the film editing process, which became much more than the simple joining of a series of progressive scenes. Seeing the photographed subject from many sides and distances not only enlivened the visual imagery, it produced a clearer sense of three-dimensional reality. Multiple angles added enormous range to the area of the stage and created an opportunity for editorial accents and dramatic emphasis or de-emphasis by visual means.

The memorable opening to Orson Welles' debut film, *Citizen Kane*, presents dark images announcing our entrance into the world of the mighty. The single word "Rosebud!" muttered from an extreme closeup of tight lips begins the mystery that follows a great man's death.

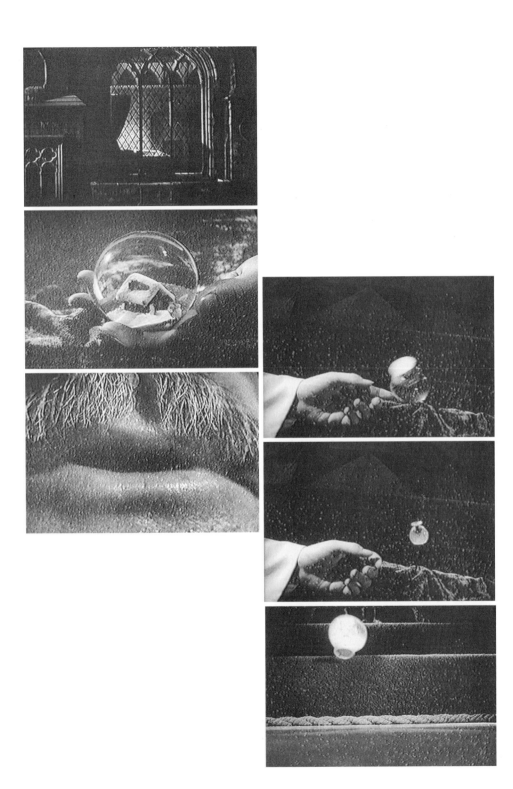

The ticking clock in *High Noon* is a metronome that beats inexorably toward the critical moment when the train arrives that carries the desperado who will join the trio of mean-visaged gunfighters waiting for him at the station. Minute by minute, image by image, the film builds tension. Marshall Kane (Gary Cooper) has been left by the townspeople to fight the gunmen alone. It is a rendezvous with death and with the conscience of the town.

This is an example of the director thinking in terms of a sequence of shots rather than the single shot, somewhat in the way a musical melody is composed of a series of notes rather than a single note.

Vorkapich criticized directors who refer to "getting that great shot" as an end in itself. He stressed that it was a better general rule to think of shots as a sequence, the director adding a film editor's as well as a cinematographer's perspective.

One of the memorable segments of film Vorkapich crafted was the Locust Plague sequence from MGM's *The Good Earth*. It remains a striking example of how multiple imagery can be combined to create a powerful reality and the screen transformed into a broad, "three-dimensional" stage. For this crucial episode in the film, a large swath of the San Fernando Valley's Chatsworth Hills was given over to planting the wheat field that the locusts would attack. Though thousands of real locusts (actually grasshoppers) were collected for closer shots, Vorkapich created the actual flying swarm and the rain of the locusts with simple iron filings on a piece of paper. The filings were shaped and moved by a magnet held beneath them and their photographed image double-printed over the landscape shots. It is worth mentioning that the use of iron filings to create an illusion of a swarm of locusts is an example of a basic principle of movie construction: The image seen need not be an exact replica of what it is supposed to be, as long as it feels as though it is. "The screen will tell" rule always applies, but the screen tells no more than it can show. Assume that the producers of *The Good Earth* had managed to figure out how to capture an enormous swarm of locusts and then released them in the Chatsworth Hills—an impractical if not dangerous idea. The principle worth stressing is that the choice of what needs to be shown and what does not need to be shown is an essential part of the craft.

The example shown in these stills is only an excerpt. Close to 100 cuts were made to create the entire sequence.

As has already been discussed, multiple images compensate with visual variety for the limits of the screen's two-dimensional surface. Does that mean that there is no place for a sustained single angle? Holding a shot does create tension, and that quality can be used expressively, even if it may cause a degree of discomfort. In the French film classic *A Man Escaped* by Robert Bresson, a prisoner held in a small cell spends months making minute scrapes between the wooden slats of his cell door in order, eventually, to remove the boards and effect his freedom.

The camera view rarely varies. The audience is trapped in the cell, like the prisoner, and suffers with him as, on several occasions, his escape preparations come close to discovery. His need and determination to escape infects the trapped audience. They and the camera lens are held with him in the small confines.

The Story of a Jazz Musician, a TV documentary I made with Paul Horn, has a sequence in which I was presented with two choices in one segment—multiple angles or a single angle. Both choices held different values, and choosing between them was difficult.

In the scene, Paul was being photographed for publicity photos. I had him sit on a stool in the otherwise bare studio. I placed my camera at the top of a ladder and moved it far enough back so that my view included Paul below me, the still photographer crouched down to the side, and an area of empty space around them. I asked Paul to improvise on his flute, knowing that the music he would create would have the plaintive quality of a lone shepherd playing to his flock. It is the kind of music that I knew particularly suits a sense of empty space.

My first approach was to create a multiple-angle situation, asking the still photographer to move around Paul and take pictures. Something that I hadn't planned on happened, which made the scene work even better: The photographer fell in with the music, clicking his camera as Paul reached the end of his musical phrases. The camera sound was loud enough to make a rhythmic accompaniment to the music. I then brought my cameras down to the same level as the still photographer and took shots of him taking his pictures, filming Paul from the angles the still photographer might be seeing him. All the shots were strong. The photographer's large lens reflected the lights, the shutter movements were visible, and the angles and lighting on Paul were dramatic. Because I had conditioned myself to think in terms of multiple shots in the editing phase, I chose to cut to those after only a brief use of the long shot as an introduction.

While the choice I made was effective, in retrospect I began to realize that something more valuable had been sacrificed. The more distant (single) angle, showing the subject's isolation in empty space, and the compatible thin line of the flute's sound provided an emotional, plaintive coloration—a subtle sense of the artist alone with his music, which, unfortunately, the other edit vitiated.

The Screen

The screen is a two-dimensional (flat) surface displaying a picture that can move and create an illusion of three dimensions.

If one defines the essential qualities of an art form as the unique characteristics that separate it from all other forms, motion and image surely define the movie. Without motion, a visible mark or color or image on a flat surface can be said to characterize many other graphic arts—drawing, painting, and still photography. Some may want to claim that these graphic arts are also without sound, and since most movies presented today are accompanied by sound, it is also a distinction of the film form. But a movie is a movie without sound. It is not a movie if it is without movement.

The characteristics unique to other art forms would be, in the case of music, for example, an organization of sounds into a matrix of relationships; in the case of sculpture, giving shape to forms in space; whereas the unique stuff of dance is in patterns of movement with the human body.

What is shared by all art forms is not the subject of discussion at this point, nor are issues of quality, such as profundity, banality, sentimentality, etc., except to state my belief that staying close to the true and unique nature of a medium gives a strong assist in fashioning a powerful, rich, and lasting experience.

Perceiving the Image:
Filmic Grammar ■■■■■■■■■■■■■■■

"Filmic" is a word that is applied rather indiscriminately by academics and film critics to anything that is seen as effective on the screen. Under this wide-ranging definition, dialogue, story, and virtually every other part of the film process is included, rendering the word nearly meaningless. I will use the word in the sense that Vorkapich used it—to define only that quality that describes the essentials of the form already discussed: motion and image.

It may be obvious that an object must be seen as distinct from its background if it is to be perceived. I was once driving my car on a remote highway in wintry conditions that were fast approaching the dangerous condition called a "white-out." With considerable apprehension, I strained to see the road ahead, but everything was becoming a flat, two-dimensional white surface (like a flat, two-dimensional screen). The road was made white by rapidly falling snow, the demarcations at the road's edge were also being covered by a white blanket. A white vaporous veil hung over the view ahead, which rapidly grew less penetrable. I considered stopping but did not want to in the middle of the road, virtually invisible to any vehicle that might be coming up behind me. If I pulled over to the road's edge I feared becoming stuck in the snow banks, where I might slowly freeze, the falling snow concealing me in a white shroud.

Rescue came with the yellow image of a snowplow, which passed me at slow speed and which I then followed. Although the plow still left the road white, the yellow outline of its shape penetrated the white veil. However, if I stayed close behind it, keeping a steady distance, I lost all sense of movement. *Nothing was changing visually in relation to me.* Of course, the sound of my engaged engine, the jostle of the road, and the logic and purpose of a moving snowplow on the road confirmed intellectually that I was indeed moving, but I remember that at some primitive level I yearned for firmer proof. The plow was the only thing I could see. I found myself regularly allowing the gap between us to change by slowing down and then catching up again, to gain a sense that we were indeed moving through space.

I trusted to faith that the plow driver's familiarity with the road gave him some ability to know his position. I was rewarded. He led me to a highway of black asphalt that other plows had kept clear of snow, and I found my way to my destination.

As I reflected on the experience, I realized that I had been given a memorable lesson in the laws of visual perception. Einstein's theory of relativity came to mind. Our physical body recognizes movement *primarily* from perceiving motion in relation to something else—in my case, the snowplow.

When one is in a stationary train alongside another train that starts to move, one experiences the convincing illusion of actually moving backward—even to the point of having the commensurate physiological response. I call this "referred motion."

Our perception of motion occurs when we notice a shifting in the spatial relationships of objects. In motion pictures, the camera's position sets up a basis for this spatial relationship. A perfect example is the famous sequence in which Fred Astaire, in a room, is seen to dance from floor to wall to ceiling to opposite wall and back to the floor (*Royal Wedding*). In setting up for that sequence, the room was designed so that it could rotate a full 360 degrees. All furniture and fixtures were constructed to stay rigidly in place. The camera was fixed to the floor so that it rotated exactly as the room did. From the camera's position, nothing in the room would appear to move in relation to it, except, of course, Astaire. He was limited only by gravity. He had only to skillfully execute his dance steps in the room that turned like a wheel. The audience was convincingly—and, of course, willingly—deluded that Fred was dancing on walls and ceiling.

If we are to acknowledge the importance of movement in mastering film technique, understanding the laws of visual perception is critical. Perception, as Gestalt psychology has made clear, is in part a psychological experience, and it is not hard to understand the evolution of certain ways of interpreting movement as part of our evolved means of survival.

Our attention is attracted to something in motion more than it is to anything stationary. Movement toward us can warn us of the threat of attack by an animal or a human. Movement away from us can mean fleeing game—food to our hunter ancestors. When the filmmaker frames his shot, he must realize that, no matter how artful his still composition, any movement within the frame takes precedence in attracting the eye. This undoubtedly stems from man's basic survival conditioning. Unlike the painter or still photographer, the motion picture maker must frame a composition with the realization that when movement occurs within that boundary, the eye will focus on it first.

Since this innate reaction to movement is a primitive, visceral, and pre-cognitive response, Vorkapich called it "the innocence of the eye." In setting up his filmmaking principles, he strove to integrate primitive with cognitive responses, to bring eye and mind into harmony.

Another primitive response is *the power of the look*. Whether primitive man was being viewed as a meal by a predator or whether the predator's look was directed at the sumptuous antelope nearby were obvious factors in survival. Whether the driver making a turn directly in front of you is cognizant of your approach or directing his attention elsewhere is also vital survival information. Which way a look is directed, therefore, has a strong psychological, pre-cognitive effect.

To enhance comprehension, our brain is eager to forge connections. It creates linkages in any chance sequence of images. This linking impulse is powerfully reinforced by the *look*. Visualize a filmed closeup of a subject staring at something or someone not visible on camera. Vorkapich stressed that our psychological impulse is to link the next cut to the look and see the thing or person in the next frame as what is being looked at. Often, however, the filmmaker is unaware or unconcerned by this linkage. He cuts to the closeup of the looker for identification or dramatic emphasis, and the next cut is to the same subject from another angle. In terms of the "innocent eye," *the looker is looking at himself*, so the film's viewer feels a brief moment of confusion.

Of course, the rationalizing brain is fast to modify its primitive response: "Oh," it tells us, "he is not looking at himself, we are seeing him from another angle!" The psychological jar is slight and rarely noticed consciously. However, Vorkapich's hope was to develop a sensitivity to this psychological visual nuance from which to create films more aligned with the primitive, innocent eye. In his hoped-for, perfected film form, such nuances would lay the rules for a filmic grammar from which a unique visual literature or poetry would develop.

The Vorkapichean wish for the development of film as a visual art has generally been diverted by the photoplay, but his concepts and rules respecting an intrinsic "picture with motion" form have nonetheless to be recognized and are to a large measure an inevitable part, if frequently only an intuitive one, of movie technique.

"All Is Not as It Seems!"
Real and Apparent Movement ■■■■■■

When movement is discussed as filmic it is necessary to stress that, of course, this movement must be apparent. The fact that an image is actually in motion is not sufficient in itself. In the white-out situation discussed previously, when I was following the snowplow from an unvarying distance, what motion there was in reality was not apparent. Nor did Fred Astaire dance up the walls. Inexperienced directors, enamored of "moving shots," will sometimes devise elaborate dolly shots (also called "tracking shots") or panoramic ("pan") shots that follow or lead a moving subject against an undifferentiated background. Great pains may have been taken to move the camera, but because of the undifferentiated background, *the desired sense of motion is lost*. Vorkapich cited as an example of this mistake the opening shot from Akira Kurosawa's otherwise excellent film *Rashoman*, in which the camera tracks the actor Toshiro Mifune walking through tall (but undifferentiated) grass. In this shot, he appears to be going through walking motions without moving. This is an example of the theory of relativity again: Something must be observed as moving in relation to something else for movement to be apparent on the screen.

Consider this situation: A man sits at the window of a moving train. The camera angle looks upward, silhouetting him against a gray (undifferentiated) sky. The train may be making a milk run at 30 miles an hour or it may be the super express going over 100, but because of the undifferentiated background, no motion is perceived. But let the angle through the window include telephone poles being passed and we have apparent motion. Our intellect conditions us to conclude that only the train is moving. The image would be exactly the same, however, if some force were able to pull the row of telephone poles past the window—but that is such an unlikely event that we immediately dismiss its possibility.

Add another element. If we see the wires connecting the telephone poles while the train is standing still, we are aware that these stationary wires form a graceful, static, hill-and-valley outline. As has been commonly experienced, however, when seen from inside a moving train, these wires constantly change themselves from a straight line into a valley shape. Our moving viewpoint has, somehow, made the wires appear to have life-like movement.

All is not as it seems. The laws of perception govern what is seen whether what is perceived is truly there.

I once took on a fascinating film project, *Flight Forms*, which required a clear sense of the laws of perception and apparent movement. The artist/sculptor Tom Van Sant had long been fascinated by the way in which the shapes of birds were a function of their ability to fly, and he had carved and cast many bird sculptures in attitudes of flight or pre-flight. His bird forms remained earthbound, however, and this led him to creating shapes that could indeed take flight. Van Sant began making a succession of beautifully painted kites. When he brought his assignment to me, he was planning for exhibitions of his kites in several European museums. He felt, however, that kites should be witnessed in flight and not merely hung from the ceiling or the walls of a museum. He decided to have a short film made of the kites in flight, which could be shown continuously during the exhibitions.

Before I began to work, Tom introduced me to his remarkable and beautiful kites in action, organizing a "fly" on the Santa Monica beach. It became clear to me that the sense of these beautiful objects soaring overhead created an emotion of exuberance and liberation. At the same time, I saw that kites actually moved very little and that most of what movement there was came from the kite's pulling up and away from the holder of the string—to the eye, growing smaller—which could hardly be expected to suggest the full experience of flight on a movie screen.

It should be pointed out that the motion picture camera, like the still camera (and, indeed, like most paintings), records views limited by the shape and size of the presentation surface, threrby having a frame of circumscribed view. The frame creates a window of limited selection. As anyone who has been moved by the beauty in the reality we see around us and has tried to capture it on film or canvas discovers, the framed "window" is not the same as 360-degree, three-dimensional reality. This fact is often frustrating to the amateur. The rules of composition, calling for an artful selection and organization within the frame, however, make use of this very limitation and are a first step in creating what has been called "the necessary aesthetic distance" separating art from reality.

The frame can also serve to make movement apparent. In much of *Flight Forms*, the sky is an undifferentiated blue. The camera slowly pans from the nose of the flying kite past the tail. On the screen, the kite is seen as moving from one position in the frame toward an edge and off.

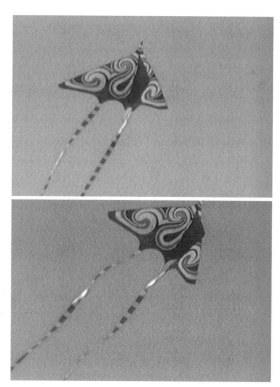

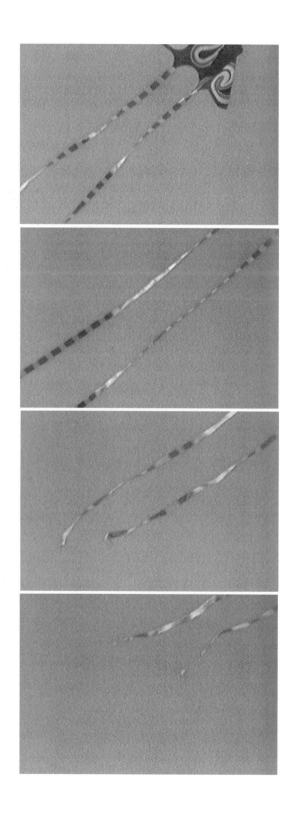

If the camera closely followed the kite as it made its tiny movements against the un-differentiated sky, keeping it within the same spot in the frame, no movement would be perceived on the screen. A kite's movement is readily apparent on the screen, however, only as it lifts off and for a few seconds is seen moving upward in relation to the ground. Though this move-ment is over quickly, when I made the film, I extended the experience by connecting a series of lift-offs of different kites, editing them together, and giving them more time on the screen by using slow motion.

Most successful was the creation of referred movement from a camera shooting from a helicopter. While a tethered kite was held still in the sky over a beautiful area of textured dunes and sea, the helicopter circled it, shooting from angles alongside and above the kite. In these shots, the kite was kept in the center of the frame, and the helicopter's movement was *borrowed* by the kite, which clearly seemed to move in relation to the ground below. Actually, it could also be said that the ground appeared to move because of the helicopter's motion, but (as in the case of the telephone poles and the train) the brain was more comfortable with the idea of the kite rather than the ground moving and made the transference.

The bird shape of the kite also suggested movement, and its sense of uninhibited flight was given an added boost by the "soaring" strains of Mozart's G Major Piano Concerto on the sound track.

Movement and Empathy ■■■■■■

The dancer depends on his movements to affect an audience—whose responses to dance have been measured as minuscule reactions of muscle connected to nerve endings. The viewer of the dance actually dances with the performer at some minuscule physiological level. The response is called kinesthesis. We don't leap when the dancer does, but nerve endings in our muscles fire away as if we are preparing to do so. Undoubtedly, this also occurs when we thrill to the acrobatic leaps of a Michael Jordan on the basketball court or we watch an Evel Knievel shoot upward on his motorcycle or follow the sudden twists of the Air Force's Blue Angels in the sky. This empathy with movement occurs in response to movement on film as well, in response to both motion occurring within the frame and the visual "kicks" created by cuts from one scene to another.

The placement of the camera and the choice of lens affect how dynamic any movement will appear to be on screen.

A *wide-angle* lens is often used to accentuate movement toward or away from the camera. The depth and width of field allow the subject in the film to grow larger as it comes toward the viewer and grow smaller as it moves away. Constant changes in the subject's size will hold the viewer's interest.

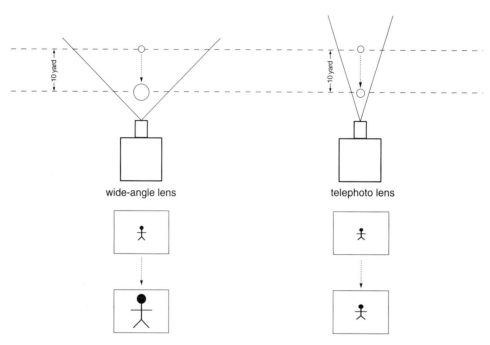

fig. 1 movement forward and backward
as emphasized by a wide-angle lens

fig. 2 movement forward and backward
de-emphasized by a telephoto lens

A striking, but not so widely used, capability of the telephoto (long) lens is the interesting way it renders side-to-side motion. I can rarely resist looking through a strong telescope that is set up on display in a shop, directing it toward close-by objects or perhaps out through the store window, perhaps through low-hanging tree branches, catching the occasional car or truck coming by on the street and, beyond that, picking up an image of pedestrians and shop windows across the street. I have been fascinated by the unexpected beauty of these everyday images brought closer together than reality would allow, offering visual kicks as they enter the field of view left to right or right to left. In this manner, many images that are separated by distances are brought together—the distances eliminated—so that we perceive them differently, as a block of images, their flattened surfaces like planes of color intermeshing. Such capability can be creatively employed in film for depicting pageantry, for example.

The telephoto can also be used to stage visual surprises by limiting the field of view. I recall some extremely effective moments in a Japanese film (title forgotten) where a tracking telephoto shot holds a close image of a charging warrior as he runs through the ranks of the enemy—his sword slashing a path. The enemy soldiers are not seen until they enter the frame for the brief moment before they are cut down, and the tracking shot never slows or leaves the charging warrior. His unimpaired forward (in this case, camera right-to-left) motion enhanced the sense of his being literally and symbolically unstoppable.

The telephoto lens has long been recognized in still and motion picture photography as a way of enhancing the human face in closeup. This is perhaps the result of it minimizing the prognathic thrust of the jaw, which may involve a primitive response to the teeth and jaw— the predator's most feared aspect. (Children have been tested to show that they instinctively prefer unfamiliar dogs with flat faces.)

The face held close to the wide-angle lens makes the contrary emphasis, increasing the distance between the mouth and back of the head, creating a more menacing, less flattering, depiction.

Movement and Intensity

The degree of loudness in music from "piano" (quiet) to "forte" (loud), the brightness and choice of color in painting, and the psychological qualities inherent in shapes in sculpture are all means of expression via levels of intensity. Similarly, movement in film excites varying degrees of visceral response. The intensity of this response follows a simple maxim: *intensity varies according to the area of screen in motion.*

fig. 1   Conventional "pretty picture" view of distant train framed by tree in foreground (very little area in motion)

fig. 2   Dynamic shot: maximum area in motion

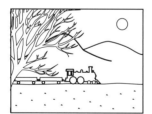

Qualities: Low intensity, but breadth and location identification

Qualities: High intensity

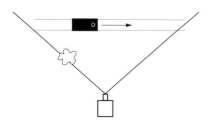

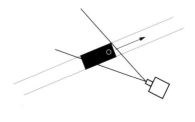

The camera angle further maximizes or minimizes that intensity.

Example 1 (fig. 1): A distant train moves horizontally across the screen. The shot is framed conventionally with a tree in the foreground, its branches extending across the top of the frame. The scene successfully renders the train in relation to its surroundings, but the actual area of screen in motion is slight and, accordingly, so is its intensity or visceral response.

Example 2 (fig. 2): The camera is set up close to the edge of the track, facing an oncoming train. As the train roars by the camera, at least one half of the screen is in motion and visceral response is great.

My intention in these examples is not to find one shot superior to the other, only to establish that each one has a different level of intensity. Both angles could be used in a series of joined shots of the train, leading toward increasing or diminishing intensity. The angle of the camera can be seen as being more or less favorable to the dynamics of movement in a shot.

The Technique of Filmic Analysis

Montage, eye-catching television commercials, and key action sequences in films demand a high level of visual intensity. It is achieved by a means Vorkapich called *filmic analysis*, which is, in general, the breakdown of complex motions into their discrete parts and the recombination of all or some of those parts to achieve the greatest emphasis or intensity. As one of the earliest and most famous creators of the Hollywood-style montage, Vorkapich led the way not only in practicing, but also, later, in teaching this visual style.

Vorkapich gave numerous assignments to his students to foster their becoming more "motion conscious." These did not involve photographic equipment, but only required making sketches, no matter how crude, of observations. He particularly stressed our need to notice the kinds of movements people made while working and by their repetition honed to an efficient and frugal simplicity. These kinds of distilled motions could be joined together in editing to achieve a structure and a filmic choreography. In the classroom, Vorkapich demonstrated how simple motions might create dance-like effects. He asked a group of students, on cue, to rise and on a following signal to sit back down. He would vary the number of participating individuals and the pace of rising and sitting. He varied the rhythms, the patterns, and the sequences, then, in at least one instance, asked everyone to sit down at once as an effective finale. The exercise developed sensitivity to all motions as possessing dance-like potential.

The following is a homework assignment I did as his student: recording the movements in a work situation. I thought if it had been filmed and edited in even a straightforward, linear form, it would have had a dance-like feeling. It also could be edited in a purely imaginative order.

Movements Involved in the Manufacture of Clay Pipe

The movements observed are part of the clay pipe manufacturing process. Dirt, which is the main ingredient in the clay mix, is brought in on special cars. A man with a pickaxe breaks the dirt into small chunks, which he shovels down a chute, where they are picked up by a small "scoop-truck" and taken to a conveyor belt that leads to the grinding and mixing areas.

1) The axe strikes the pile of dirt. Chunks break loose and fall. A cloud of dust rises and curls.

2) The shovel scoops up the dirt and throws it down the chute.

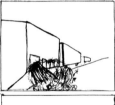

3) The dirt pours out of the chute and hits the earth. A pile of dirt builds up. A cloud of dust rises and whirls around.

4) The scoop-truck arrives with the scoop carried high. As it approaches the pile, the scoop is dropped until it is flush with the ground.

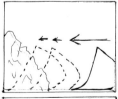

5) In a series of jogs, the scoop is pushed deep into the dirt pile.

6) The scoop is rotated, its mouth turning upward, and its arm is raised high.

7) The scoop, with its mouth now facing upward, is given a short, very abrupt jog to settle the dirt evenly within it.

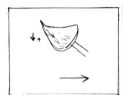

8) The scoop-truck backs up in an arc to the left (viewed from the top) and then pulls out, arcing to the right.

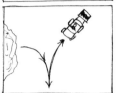

9) The scoop rotates; the dirt spills into a trough that feeds a conveyor belt. The dirt spreads on the conveyor belt, which carries it to the grinder.

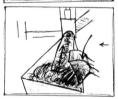

10) On the other side of the trough is a pit containing another variety of dirt. A man in the pit throws shovelsful into the trough. His shovel describes half an arc. The dirt continues the arc to a point, then drops into the trough.

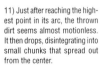

11) Just after reaching the highest point in its arc, the thrown dirt seems almost motionless. It then drops, disintegrating into small chunks that spread out from the center.

12) As the dirt hits the pile, it sprays outward. Dust curls up and around it.

The Clay Pipe Machine

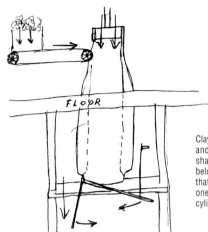

Clay clods are fed into the cylinder and compressed into the proper shape by the piston. On the floor below, a man works two levers: one that disengages the equipment and one that lowers the pipe from the cylinder.

On the other side of the machine is an assembly line of three men. The first man (A) slips a platform and base under the pipe. The second man (B) stamps a trademark on the pipe and pushes it down a platform of rollers. The third man (C) cuts a small section off the top of the pipe with a jig and then pushes the pipe onto a waiting dolly.

1) A lever is swung to the left to disengage pipe.

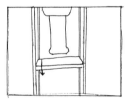

4) The pipe stops, but the crossbar beneath it continues to travel down a little farther.

2) Another lever is swung to the right to lower pipe out of cylinder.

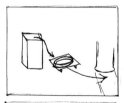

5) A platfrom and a base is swung under the pipe in an arc-like motion.

3) The pipe slowly drops out of the cylinder.

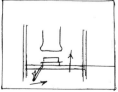

6) The lever is swung back to the right, and the crossbar rises, moving the base up into the pipe.

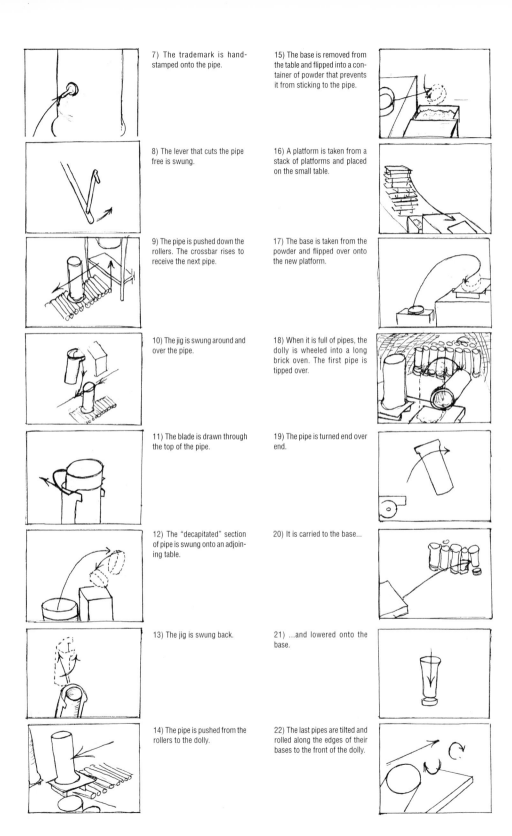

7) The trademark is hand-stamped onto the pipe.

8) The lever that cuts the pipe free is swung.

9) The pipe is pushed down the rollers. The crossbar rises to receive the next pipe.

10) The jig is swung around and over the pipe.

11) The blade is drawn through the top of the pipe.

12) The "decapitated" section of pipe is swung onto an adjoining table.

13) The jig is swung back.

14) The pipe is pushed from the rollers to the dolly.

15) The base is removed from the table and flipped into a container of powder that prevents it from sticking to the pipe.

16) A platform is taken from a stack of platforms and placed on the small table.

17) The base is taken from the powder and flipped over onto the new platform.

18) When it is full of pipes, the dolly is wheeled into a long brick oven. The first pipe is tipped over.

19) The pipe is turned end over end.

20) It is carried to the base...

21) ...and lowered onto the base.

22) The last pipes are tilted and rolled along the edges of their bases to the front of the dolly.

Sensitivity to motion leads directly to Vorkapich's principle of filmic analysis: *break down more or less complex motions into single-motion components, choose the most dynamic angle for each component, and then combine them into one sequence.*

VISUAL ANALYSIS

Different angles of simple movements can be joined together to create
a strong visceral effect

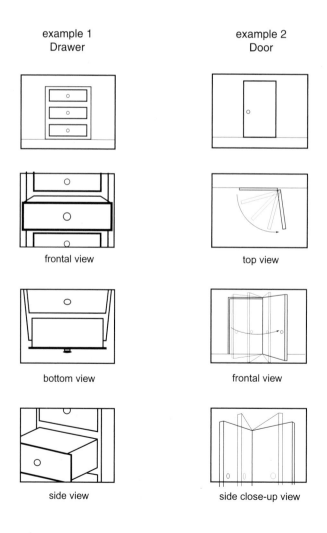

example 1 Drawer	example 2 Door
frontal view	top view
bottom view	frontal view
side view	side close-up view

Vorkapich would remark upon how often simplified motions evoked simple geometric shapes. Opening a book formed a half circle in space; opening or closing a door, depending on the angle, could be seen as a "wipe" of the screen; opening or shutting a drawer was the enlarging or diminishing of a rectangle.

The filmmaker can separate these motions by angle, recombine them as he wills in editing, and add music or sound devices. Closeness or distance, the amount of intensity, can be controlled and a film dance can indeed become possible. Using the realistic "linear" patterns of the motions of the subject one is filming to start with, then rearranging those motions into unexpected relationships—utilizing movement for its own sake—an abstract dance-like form can be created. The more this filmic experience deviates from the literal, the more it can approach the pure aspects of dance. This is not to say that the images should in any way be altered to make them unreal. The exciting thing about this film dance is its unique ability to represent two different realities at once: the reality of the actual motions of the subject and something else (perhaps surprising and emotional) that exists only for the viewer—a dance hymn to the filmic process itself.

Probably the best-known example of visual (filmic) analysis is the famous shower scene in Hitchcock's *Psycho*. The murder of Janet Leigh in the shower by the knife-wielding Anthony Perkins is much more than a recording of the horrific event. It is an elaborate orchestration of images and movement, an analytical breakdown of the physical act of murder into its component elements (images), each image chosen for its simplicity and suggestive power, and then reassembled into a coherent form.

The shower scene, which differs markedly in technique from the rest of the film, is created in the intense style of a Vorkapich montage and is so extraordinarily effective in underlining the horror of the moment that it is considered a memorable piece of filmmaking in itself, a work of art even apart from the noteworthy film. This scene is also a prime example of *telling a story by indirection*, which I will discuss later. The parts are shown, the whole is implied, the audience's imagination fills the gaps and is therefore part creator of the scene.

There has been some controversy as to whether the shower scene was actually directed by Hitchcock or by Sol Bass, a filmic artist whose best-known work was in creating daring and original opening titles for many motion pictures. Because of the Vorkapichean style of the shower sequence and my recollections of Bass's attendance at the classes Vorkapich offered at his home after he left USC, I tend to believe that Sol, who worked on *Psycho*, may have made, in the very least, a significant contribution to the shower sequence.

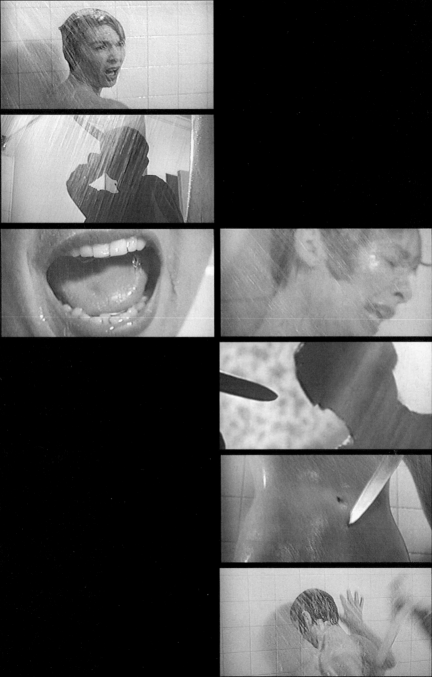

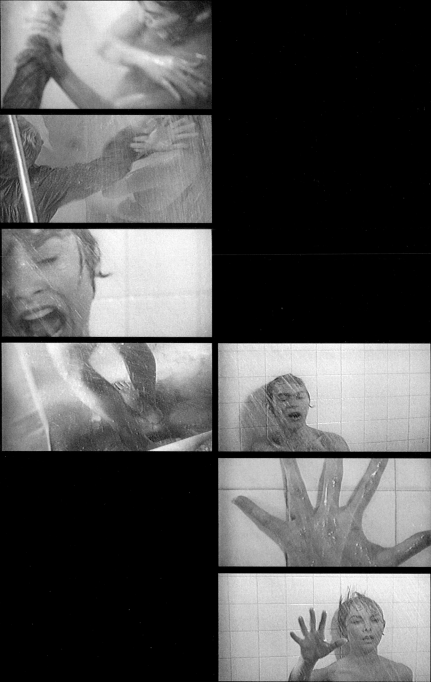

The Technique of Filmic Analysis

One of Vorkapich's very first students was painter, film editor, and film director John Hoffman. The two met at MGM, and Vorkapich brought Hoffman to USC to teach. Hoffman, who was an enthusiastic champion of Vorkapich's film theories, unfortunately felt compelled to resign in support of Vorkapich's resignation.

Among other fine pieces of work, Hoffman was responsible for the brilliant earthquake sequence (which Vorkapich much admired) in the film *San Francisco*. Even from these few stills one can observe similarities in the style of visual analysis between the *San Francisco* earthquake and the *Psycho* shower sequences.

Hoffman's filmic earthquake is a masterpiece of cinematic art, from its depiction of the first rumblings of the tremors to the end of the quake's destructive shaking, utilizing the visual analysis of a wagon's destruction by the toppling ornamental statue of a Greek god. The wagon is smashed in a series of shots that end on a single severed wagon wheel pirouetting like a dancer before slowing to fall on its side, quivering until all motion ceases. This visually inventive structural punctuation—ending a noisy action scene with the contrast of static images and quiet—is described later in this book in reference to the Bolivia Battle in *Butch Cassidy and the Sundance Kid*.

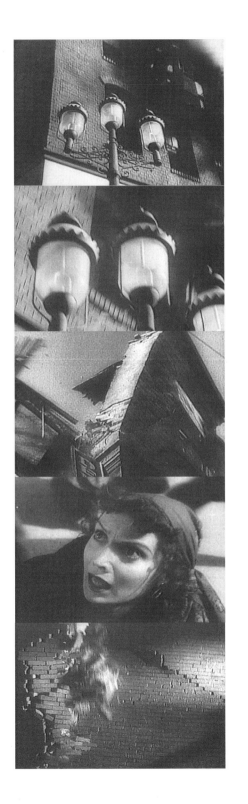

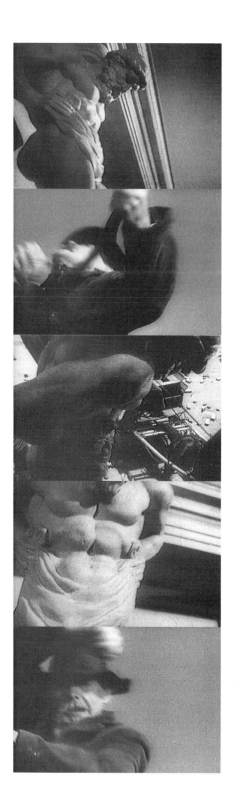

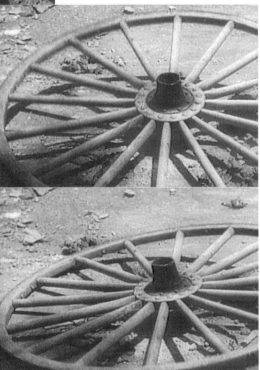

James Whales' *The Bride of Frankenstein* is a brilliant sequel to a horror classic. This film has a fine example of how filmic analysis can heighten the experience of a moment. The key idea in the film is Doctor Frankenstein's decision to provide his monster with a female companion. Most of the film sets the stage for the meeting of the monster and his newly created bride by describing the difficulties in reaching this critical moment. It is a moment of surprising poignancy—the monster in his innocent eagerness drives his female equivalent, wonderfully realized by Elsa Lancaster, to a point of absolute terror, and their first and only date is a debacle. The filmic treatment of this climactic scene can be clearly seen to realize the dramatic need.

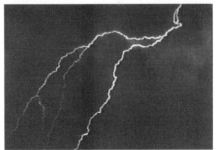

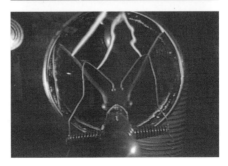

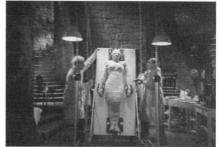

The filmic analysis style provides the editor with a breadth of material that can be combined in unexpected ways—sometimes into a form that is different and perhaps superior to the one planned for. I once directed a film sequence with the following storyline (silent save for music to be added later) for the use of an advanced film class. It provides a case in point.

> A young woman comes into a restaurant and waits at a table for her date. Time passes. She orders wine and drinks a glass. More time passes, more drinks. She becomes increasingly self-conscious that men at other tables are observing her being stood up. She drinks too much. Very drunk, she tries to get up, falls back onto the chair with her upper body stretching out on the table top, her hand knocking over her glass of wine, and passes out.

I deliberately directed this simple dramatic idea with an unusual degree of filmic analysis. Each of my thirteen students received copies of the raw footage and the assignment to choose a piece of music and edit the material to it in any way he or she saw fit.

The results were a delight to me. The unusually great amount of coverage I shot facilitated thirteen very different interpretations. No two sequences were alike: some were comic, some sad, several deviated quite sharply from the storyline but made their own effective statement. Mainly, the coverage allowed silent material to compensate for its lack of dialogue with a compelling visual interest.

Unfortunately, we cannot screen the sequences in a book, but still photos can at least demonstrate the visually analytic nature of the material.

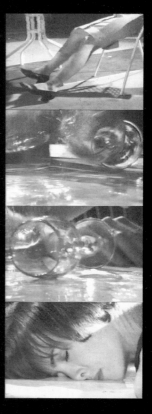

▪▪▪▪Contrasting Motion With Stillness

Ludwig Von Beethoven is credited with the unforgettable—but initially alarming—opinion that the pause was the most eloquent moment in music. The pause seems to allow the active mode that preceded it to resonate and to "play out" as a sound retained by our memory. The expressiveness of movement in film, too, can be best appreciated when moments of rest follow. The fury of a battle, for example, can achieve an eloquence when it is followed by a totally quiet scene of the litter of dead left in its wake. In filming the contrast, the filmmaker might want to consider heightening the sense of the total immobility of death by keeping the camera static. A cessation of movement is like a period at the end of a sentence. It brings an event to a close.

In *Butch Cassidy and the Sundance Kid*, the two expatriate Americans in Bolivia are reluctantly drawn into a gun battle by a gang of local "banditos." Forced to fire, Butch and Sundance do so first and at a furious pace, wiping out the seven Bolivians before they can even draw their guns. As one bandito after another is hit, they begin to fall in slow motion, adding a balletic quality to the moment. The heightened awareness brought on by slow motion is often very similar to the way people who go through moments of real physical crisis report experiencing such events. It seems to be the exactly right technique for depicting such moments in a motion picture.

There then follows a series of static shots of the Bolivians' bodies with the stirred-up clouds of dust drifting over them. Butch and Sundance are also filmed in a series of static shots as they record the consequences of their actions.

Geography and the Window ▮▮▮▮▮▮

At one time or another, nearly every filmmaker has to confront the not-so-simple problem of rendering a clear sense of an actual geographic place on a movie screen. A common approach that attempts to give some sense of a physical location is the pan shot. As the lens moves past distant objects, however, there is little spatial distinction between them, and a flattening effect is created, weakening the suggestion of three dimensions. Furthermore, the actual arc of the camera's motion translates on the screen as an endless straight line. Even when the camera completes a 360-degree pan, the return to the starting point comes almost as a surprise to the innocent eye.

A moving camera or dolly, though, reinforces the illusion of three dimensions because the camera moves from the front to the side of objects it passes. But, again, it is insufficient for establishing a complete picture of the overall geography. The best answer would probably be to have a 360-degree screen that surrounds an audience. Not a practical solution.

The problem of exactly representing a real area on screen is probably not solvable practically. What must be kept in mind is what a movie is good at doing and what it is not. The window or frame may limit the rendering of actual geography, but in compensation, it serves as a stimulus to the director's imagination and his visual invention. The ancient Greeks said that art is always created within chains. These limitations or chains have to be confronted constantly in the complex, expensive picture-making process. I suggest that the filmmaker psychologically prepare himself for these challenges and welcome the stimulus to his artistry.

The fact is that a movie creates its own geography within the frame. This is most evident in the issue of "screen direction" that every director has to learn to deal with. ("Screen direction" refers to the generally accepted rules governing our spatial perception of two or more objects or persons on screen.) Again, it is vital to take into account the consequences of the "look." Such terms as "screen right" and "screen left" replace normal descriptions of direction. As is now generally known, if we are in a closeup of someone holding a normal conversation with another person to the camera's right, the subsequent cut is to the image of the other person in the dialogue looking camera left. The term "stage line" is used to suggest an imaginary line that must not be crossed by the camera's point of view if the illusion of the two people looking at each other is to be maintained.

Two people in conversation: stage line and reversing screen direction

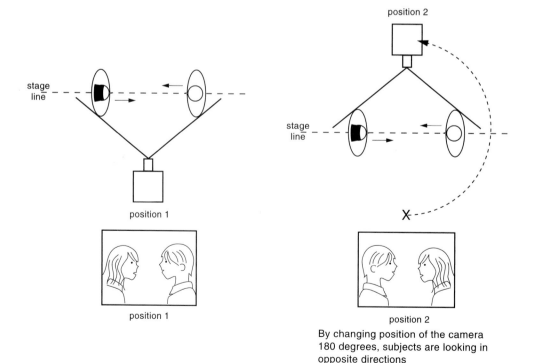

position 1

position 2
By changing position of the camera 180 degrees, subjects are looking in opposite directions

If, for whatever reason, the director moves his camera across the imaginary stage line to cover the second person, that person will be seen looking camera right, not left, i.e., the same direction as the subject in the first shot.

The concept of a stage line is not to be taken too literally. The important principle to note is how the movie frame creates its own geography and is a further illustration of the power of the "look."

The Look: Motion Picture Continuum ■ of the Battle Sequence in *Joan of Arc*

Vorkapich's last Hollywood assignment before changing his career to become an educator was to design and direct the battle scenes for the 20th Century Fox version of *Joan of Arc*, starring Ingrid Bergman and directed by Victor Fleming. Vorkapich was summoned to create a subtly stylized major battle that would fit the legend of the miraculously inspired peasant girl. As was his custom, Vorkapich drew elaborate storyboards of the action he would later direct and edit. These images reveal his strengths at envisioning striking imagery and his design for visual clarity in the way they would be edited. Massive battle scenes in movies can easily fall into massive confusion. Armies mill about, encircle, surge, and retreat. Who's winning, who's losing? Who's who in any given moment on the screen can confuse an audience.

To achieve clarity in this scene, Vorkapich paid strong attention to screen direction, and his storyboards assisted him greatly in maintaining a consistency of screen direction during the actual shooting.

Joan's forces always move and look to screen left; the English forces look and move screen right.

Screen direction is not always simple to maintain. Many directors have lost their ways during the filming of complicated scenes: Opposing armies move in the same direction; lovers allegedly looking at each other end up looking in the same direction (as if they were both looking at someone else).

A group sitting around a round table can present innumerable problems, and the editor's freedom to make editorial choices can become severely restricted by the direction a character is looking, at whom he is looking, and where the camera is placed at that moment. A round table scene is a situation that should probably best be laid out carefully in advance, preplanned from beginning to end.

More than two characters seated around a table

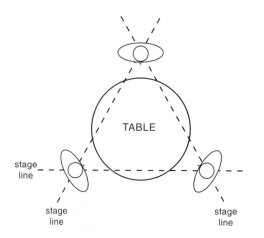

There are now three stage lines. If the camera is moved, any move across any one line will reverse at least one character's screen direction.

Reversing screen direction can be avoided:

1) If the camera's change of position is seen as a moving shot;

2) If the characters in scene are viewed changing position;

3) If a cut is made to a closeup of a character as he changes the direction of his gaze.

Visual Incidentals: Moving or Stationary Camera

The dolly or traveling shot has its visual and visceral charms, and the pan shot has the virtue of establishing the distance between visual elements to the right and left of one another, but both shots preclude making changes in editing. Dolly and pan shots end jarringly if they are cut away from while the camera is in motion. (An exception, however, is when the next cut is to another similar moving shot, preferably moving at the same speed.) However, more or less stationary shots can, if necessary, be deleted or their order of sequence or length changed pretty much at will.

The zoom lens merely brings the center of the screen forward and, unlike the dolly, diminishes rather than enhances the sense of three dimensions. Since the exact same point of view is maintained throughout the zoom, its effect is comparable to the enlargement of a still photograph. The flattening draws attention to itself and takes the viewer out of the world within the frame. The zoom's flattening effect, however, can be minimized or completely disguised if it is used in conjunction with the pan of a moving subject.

If the horizon is visible in a shot, the director should be certain that the camera angle does not cause the horizon line to tilt. In our everyday experience, a straight horizon line is a well-established constant. Any deviation from that yields a disturbing dislocation of our senses.

When the horizon is not visible in a scene, a tilt may be of little concern unless there are objects present with a strong perpendicular reference, such as a stand of straight trees, skyscrapers, or people standing. Of course, The Leaning Tower of Pisa might be an exception to the rule.

A horizon line in motion, such as one rising and falling, is also physiologically unsettling, enough so as to cause the viewer nausea. The rising and falling is often the result of shooting a scene from aboard a rocking boat or some other moving conveyance. I would argue that this is not the best way to make an audience share the experience of seasickness, even if it might be deemed as suiting the scene. If the characters are meant to portray seasickness, let the audience participate via psychological empathy (keeping an aesthetic distance) rather than undergoing a similar physiological condition.

One should always be aware that the camera lens sees things differently from the brain-connected eye. The camera mechanically records every detail of the event it photographs. The human eye is selective, picking up just enough pieces of the picture to make a whole from the parts. This process of whole-making, called "gestalt," limits the excess of stimuli that can cause confusion, conserves energy, and protects the viewer from dizziness. But the camera, with its literalness, forces the eye/brain into looking at it all, into "seeing" it the same way the camera does.

The screen image will not resemble the way things look to the naked eye and may create a disconcerting instability if a cameraman shoots while walking with the camera on his shoulder (unless he uses some form of stabilizing gear to smooth out the bumps of his steps). French filmmaker Jean Luc Goddard's much-heralded expression of the New Wave movement, his film *Breathless*, was accorded much acclaim for his constant use of the handheld camera. Vorkapich demurred and found the shaking images annoying, a technique that incessantly drew attention to itself and, thereby, in this case, distracted from the film's story.

I would not want to preclude all uses of the handheld camera (and I believe that its jarring effect in *Breathless* was perhaps desired). When it is following a person walking or running and the subject fills up a large area of the frame, the curse of the jagged shaking is lessened. The shaking of the camera and of the moving subject to a large extent cancel one another. An image stabilizer, like the Steadicam for handheld shooting, overcomes this problem to a large extent, although it somewhat inhibits the dexterity of the simple handheld camera.

The mobility of going "handheld" allows for quick adjustments to the unforeseen in the action. This rough style may feel less deliberately set up and, therefore, suitable for scenes reaching for documentary realism. (Viewers automatically associate this style with real situations, like newsreels and home movies, which it resembles at least superficially.)

The handheld camera can be taken readily into crowded spaces as when, in The Battle of the Wilderness segment of my film *The Surrender at Appomattox*, I ordered my actor/troops to march directly through bramble, vine, and bush to capture a sense of the denseness of the wilderness area. I ordered a path that penetrated into very dense growth that was extremely difficult to traverse. The actual troops in the Civil War battle likely would not have chosen quite so difficult a path, but the camera exaggerates empty space,

so a scene must be *packed with visual detail* to effectively suggest congestion. The handheld camera fought the undergrowth like my weary actors, pushing vines and branches aside, then catching them whipping back as they struck the lens. A soldier was glimpsed swatting a bug on his neck, another stumbling—the scene appeared random as a combat camera might have caught it, unplanned and more convincing than a slickly controlled sequence.

Reverse Motion

One of the earliest discoveries made with film technique was the possibility of reversing an action. Anyone who has begun to play with film editing has at one time or another taken pleasure in this phenomenon of getting an action to reverse itself by running the film backward. Perhaps some underlying sense of power resides in our ability to reverse time in this way.

An action shot can begin from a position of perfect rest. In the reverse mode, a shot ends where it actually began—in a position of perfect rest. Coming to a stop in nature rarely, if ever, ends in perfect rest. Even a near-perfect dismount from the parallel bars by an expert gymnast has a degree of wobble.

Reverse action was employed in the early screen comedies, but exhausted its interest with time. The technique was employed interestingly by Sergei Eisenstein in his film classic *Alexander Nevsky*.

In *Alexander Nevsky*, grim and superbly efficient warriors, the Teutonic Knights, invade Russia. They encounter unexpected resistance from Nevsky's Russian forces and make a momentary retreat on the battlefield, grouping into their defensive phalanx, which appears to be an invincible fortress of shields lining up machine-like, without a misalignment or jostle and in perfect symmetry. Their long lances, too, lower to face the enemy in perfect unison. They appear to be a superbly disciplined war machine, but such perfect meshing of shields and of lances could never have occurred naturally. It was, however, simple to effect with reverse motion by shooting the action forward from the position of perfect alignment, then printing the action in reverse.

Three Dimensions and the World
Within the Frame

For dramatic purposes, directors sometimes shoot scenes at askew angles, perhaps to give the sense of something not being quite right or to add a desired element of menace. The technique, if extreme, may draw attention to itself and draw the audience away from being involved solely with what the film is about.

Normally, an audience gives itself over willingly to the imaginary life within the movie frame and is not happy to be reminded that all is artifice. This, of course, is why fictional characters pretend an audience is not there and, except for rare comic or stylistic purposes, do not address the screen viewer by looking or talking directly into the camera. Many screen techniques draw attention to themselves: the already-mentioned zoom lens, the old iris in and out, the hard-edge wipes, and the excessive use of the handheld camera. Even swish pans, which once were commonplace, have been largely abandoned for the reason that they draw attention to the screen's flat surface and tend, therefore, to bring the audience out of their immersion in another "three-dimensional" world within the movie's frame.

One can argue that the three-dimensional illusion is an inevitable partner with motion, that in nature, motion cannot be readily imagined as occurring in less than three dimensions. But dealing with a three-dimensional illusion on a two-dimensional surface also has an advantage. An entire range of possibilities created in the editing process—cutting effects, dissolves, etc.—do not seem to work well in the few "3-D" films that have been made. Every cut in 3-D films seems to create an abrupt visual dislocation that resists linkage. It seems that the third dimension of depth requires too much adjustment of the viewer's sense of perspective. I am not condemning 3-D films per se (pretty much a non-issue), but hoping to increase the awareness and appreciation for the advantages of a three-dimensional illusion on a two-dimensional plane.

The director should join the cinematographer in planning his angles to emphasize the three-dimensional. A common defect with a neophyte's direction is allowing the actors' movements to trap them against a wall. A lack of depth makes for an uninteresting image, which is sometimes also uncomfortable to watch.

A sense of space is best created not only by a distant backdrop, like a view of a city or a mountain range, but by setting up middle-ground *space markers*—objects or people within the eye's trajectory—which give us a means for the comparative measure of distance. One can set up an action that occurs beyond an open doorway, for example, and the doorframe becomes a space marker.

EMPHASIZING DEPTH AND THREE DIMENSIONS

strong perspective

Through a door and beyond

Fantasy of the Filmic Eye

Even the human eye with the best vision has its limits. It cannot see unaided at the micro-scopic or telescopic level. It cannot readily accentuate visual detail by isolating the desired image from its surrounding area. The moving picture camera, however, can take our vision with it into places we never see, and/or see common places in ways we never have before.

The human eye unaided cannot slow the speed of ballet dancers so that their very muscles quiver to the music, as in *Pas de deux*, Norman McLaren's film for the Canadian Film Board. The human eye does not usually enter a world that shines with the brilliance of crystalline formations splitting, shattering, and ramming or see growing shards of brilliant, multicolored crystals acting like life forms, transforming into new shapes and colors, as in Carroll Ballard and Gary Goldsmith's *Crystallization.* The human eye may see a field of wheat tugging in the wind—this way, that way—but it cannot see, as the camera can by selection, a sea of grain and nothing else, a world of storm and stress and waves trying to escape the wind's lashing.

The naked eye is not apt to concentrate on an isolated patch of oil scum floating on water and see it as palettes of color, catching and twisting the reflection of nearby ships into beautiful, independent, organic things seemingly alive with their own pulsations. But the camera isolates, subtracts, abstracts, turns reality into non-figurative art.

Suggesting Life Beyond the Frame ■■■■

The fact that the frame limits our view can be used to create an implied, adjacent reality—an off-screen area not seen, but suggested. A window can be shuttered or a door closed, locking the actors inside their set, or be unshuttered or be opened as a portal to a street and a life beyond. The sense of a larger world beyond the frame maintains the perception of a scene's reality and atmosphere. Sounds whose sources are not visible can be added: a ticking clock in a next room, horses' hooves galloping by outside the window, the sound of a streetcar approaching and passing or coming to a stop, traffic or crowd noise, church bells, a distant fog horn, fragments of speech from passersby outside a window—suggesting life beyond the stage.

What is allowed to be seen at or near the edge of the frame can also direct our awareness to something else going on outside the frame. The background, too, can intimate diversity and actions not clearly seen, only glimpsed in the background, where they suggest a fuller, three-dimensional reality. Every director should be conscious that the space for his action is not only the stage behind the footlights or that "stage" within the camera's view.

By necessity, I implied life beyond the frame many times when I made a number of simulated documentaries for television. These films were constructed to appear as real events captured by documentary or newsreel motion-picture cameras even though, in all but one case, these technical devices did not exist as yet in the periods being represented. Actors were made to seem to be actual people who might have been present at the locations being filmed. Two of these films dealt with events during the Civil War; another recreated the story of four Army volunteers from Harvard in World War I. The fact that the budgets for these films were extremely modest made it critical to be able to imply a grander scope of activity than I could make visible.

In the Civil War film *Lincoln, Trial by Fire*, a unit of the Union Army is brought to parade in front of the then-popular General McClellan, who is seen looking out at them from a second-story window of his home. I had fewer than 25 soldiers in uniform. I utilized an old movie trick: After the lead soldiers had passed in front of the lens, I had them run around in back of the camera and join up with the tail of the column to pass in front of the lens again, and so on.

A useful camera technique employs the special capacity of the telephoto lens, which, like the telescope, causes subjects extending backward away from the lens to appear closer together than they are. In the Civil War epic *The Surrender at Appomattox*, General Ulysses S. Grant has to ride by a group of soldiers who raise their caps to cheer him. Again faced with few total actors, I trained a telephoto lens on a small soldier group, knowing that the lens would squeeze them tightly together, creating a crowded look. I made sure no space showed to the side of the group, even cutting off parts of the soldier's bodies who stood at the edges of the frame. Not showing the edge of a group creates a feeling that there are still more men who are not seen. When seeing a clean edge, on the other hand, the mind is apt to assume that the number is limited to what is visible.

Parts can represent the whole, a few can suggest themselves as part of the many. When the camera pans away from one on-camera activity to disclose a peripheral activity, it begins to suggest that there is activity all around. Imagine, for example, a camera leaving a group of soldiers as they sing a song, panning to the left and revealing a scene of other soldiers eating around a campfire. A single soldier then enters from camera right to take a burning twig out of the campfire and light a cigarette. Imagine that other persons enter the frame from camera left carrying armfuls of firewood. The sound of whinnying horses mixes with the song off screen. A voice, presumably a sergeant's, calls out drill commands in the further distance. The sound of marching boots nears and recedes.

We have not seen the firewood being gathered, the horses, the soldiers drilling, but we imagine it happening off screen. What has been created is the atmosphere of a soldier's camp—a total geographic space of *many* people rather than isolated setups of a handful that we may feel exist just for the camera. The director's job is to time the camera movement and where actions intersect so that they flow smoothly, appearing unprompted while implying active space outside of our view.

Caution: Sometimes this "choreographing" of camera and intersecting movements can work too efficiently, and the intended realistic, happenstance quality is undermined. A certain roughness may be necessary to keep a natural feeling. Achieving too efficient and geometric a movement pattern can be a pitfall. Documentary director Leo Hurwitz once cautioned me that in attempting to choreograph men doing harvest work, I should not forget that "some dirt always comes along with dug-up potatoes," i.e., allow for the less-than-perfect rough edges. He had a point.

Another approach to implying more than is seen utilizes the natural interferences that partially obscure a wide view. My *Appomattox* film referred to above covered a time in the war when there were frequent battles. It was unnecessary to show them all. The one chosen, called The Battle of the Wilderness in the historical records, was representative, but it was also the most readily filmable in light of our resources. In the Wilderness Battle, the combatants were forced to fight in dense woods where they were often invisible to one another. What couldn't be seen not only made the atmosphere ominous, but also made the production executive in charge of budget very happy. (See stills on pages 77-79.)

The smoke of battle was another way to obscure vision and save manpower. I used the outpourings from smoke canisters to obscure a portion of the action. Enemy soldiers emerged, then disappeared into the haze, and sometimes appeared again dangerously close. The obscured vision conveyed great tension and fear just because much was unseen and therefore unknown.

I strove for what I believed felt real rather than concerning myself unduly with literal historical detail, but accurate historical detail did most often guarantee that the image felt right. I tried to take into account a modern audience's degree of visual sophistication. We have been flooded by real images on the news, in combat footage from actual fighting fronts and from images gleaned on the city's streets as encountered by real-life policemen. The average television viewer may not always know why something feels real, but he can sense when it does. For example, in traditional war movies, the camera is often placed at a three-quarter angle in *front* of a soldier while he is in a combat situation, firing at an enemy. Why not? It shows the combatant's expression and the angle is dynamic. In actuality, as real war footage has conditioned us, the combat cameraman keeps behind the firing troops so as not to expose himself needlessly to enemy fire. My pseudo combat cameraman, therefore, stayed behind the troops. If the troops were routed and had to retreat full speed, my cameraman ran with them (though fortunately he kept his camera running).

In real documentary filming, one is not always able to get a perfectly clean angle. One device I used deliberately was making a shot or two appear as if stolen through a window. I found that the takes where the images were partly obscured by a reflection in the glass or by a piece of window segment frame were more convincing as reality. As was quoted before, "In reality, some dirt always comes along with dug-up potatoes."

In my *Appomattox* film, three Union soldiers huddle, trying to load their guns as they scan the smoke-covered landscape, fearfully trying to locate the unseen foe. This shot served as sharp contrast with the furious pace of the battle that just preceded. Only the single sound of the ramrod pushing the charge into the barrel is heard. The sudden near silence and the smoke-obscured view heightened an ominous foreboding. The audience collaborated in the moment's tension via its own imagination.

Leaving something unseen—deliberately withholding a perfect view—was a technique used by Roman Polanski in the scene in *Rosemary's Baby* in which Rosemary (Mia Farrow) goes into labor with what we will learn later is her witch child. The secret witch character played by Ruth Gordon leaves Rosemary to go into the next room to summon the other witches by telephone. From Rosemary's point of view through an open door, only Gordon's back is seen sitting on a chair while she leans toward a telephone held out of frame; her words, heard by Rosemary and the audience, are mere murmurs. It is an elusive nuance consistent with a story in which the facts are only vaguely hinted at, and never learned until the very end. The truth is always just beyond Rosemary's hearing and seeing.

The Isolation of the Closeup

The closeup has many uses. We see an actor's facial communication clearly, creating intensity and achieving intimacy by close proximity. The closeup, when entered via a "jump" cut
to the suddenly enlarged image, is a point of emphasis. The closeup, by filling the frame,
also has the effect of visually separating an individual's face from its immediate surroundings. This subtle detachment heightens the audience's sense of the subject's inner processes: thought, suspicion, doubt, or budding love—a pleasure not yet expressed or ecstasy when it is fully being realized. The closeup may keep us from knowing what may be
happening in the subject's immediate area. The closeup can set up the audience for surprise
when the surroundings are revealed again. The wider scene can now contain a new element—a character or event that will change the potential of the scene, e.g., the arrival of a
threat, a lover, a rival, etc. It can also be used as a form of transitional device. One anticipates
that the cut away from the closeup to the wider scene will reveal the *same wide scene* we
have left for the closeup. Instead, it is possible to cut to a new location entirely, adding an
element of excitement through surprise.

When the closeup is part of a pan, the subject can be made to occupy most of the frame
while the background is barely revealed. In this way, the pan may take on a quality not too
different from that offered by a tracking shot, allowing for a sense of motion while concentrating on the actor's inner reflections. At the end of my *Appomattox* film I wanted to see
General Grant on horseback with his standard-bearer on a horse behind him, flag unfurled—
the war behind him—riding off before the fadeout (symbolically, into the future). For this
purpose, I wanted to hold Grant's image and expression on the screen for a long take. A

tracking shot was beyond our technical capabilities in a wooded area, so I chose instead to effect a 360-degree pan, including filming a piece at the start, before the camera turned, and at the end, after the 360 degrees had been executed. Grant's image remained in only slightly varying degrees of closeness to the camera, allowing the easy maintenance of focus as he led his horse in a loop with the camera as its center point. Tree trunks and low-hanging branches whizzed by in front and behind him, conveying the sense of movement. But, as desired, there was no clear sense that he was executing a perfect loop for the camera.

The 360-degree pan as an equivalent of a tracking shot:

360-DEGREE PAN: GRANT'S 360-DEGREE RIDE

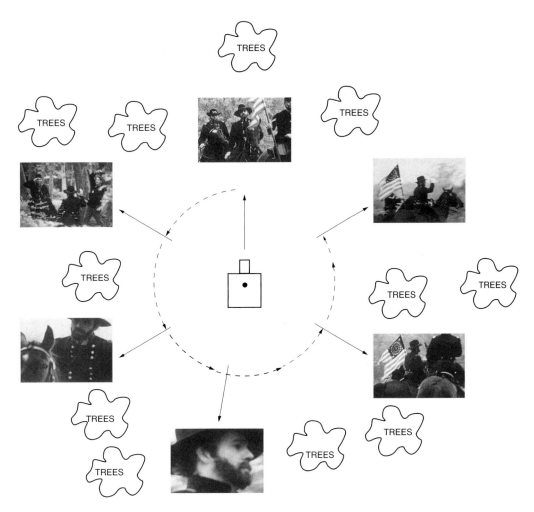

Space and the Wider Angle

The area of screen showing motion allows for a structure of either increasing or diminishing intensity. Control comes from evaluating the area of screen in motion in a sequence of shots.

The screen appears to welcome spatial variety, and the breathing room provided by the wide shot is an essential part of the scale of gradations the filmmaker can use expressively. The closeup is often used at a scene's dramatic peak; the long or wide shot is often a break or relaxation of intensity—the breath in between peaks.

Case in point: I watched a very informative documentary on the life of bees, but I felt claustrophobic after having my nose pushed into the beehive for virtually the length of the program. (Of course, I could have hit the remote and watched Clint Eastwood ride into town or out of town against a backdrop of sparse western spaces, taken a deep breath, and returned to the beehive.)

A scene emphasizing space often serves as a movie's beginning or ending. Traditionally, an opening wide shot establishes a locale. The cowboy riding into town from the outskirts or a train or plane arriving induce a sense of a beginning. Leaving town can suggest an ending. Charlie Chaplin playing the Little Tramp is seen at the end of the old one-reeler walking his characteristic walk down the road and away.

In director Carole Reed's *The Third Man,* a particularly effective setting is used twice: Close to the beginning and, memorably, at the end is a long view down a straight road that is lined by pruned bare trees in winter outside of post-World War II, Vienna, Austria. It leads from the graveyard where Harry Lime, an American who has become a local gangster (played by Orson Welles), has just been buried, the first time with someone else's body substituting for his, the second time for real.

Alida Valli plays Lime's loyal—in death and life—girlfriend who is present at both internments. An illegal refugee and poor, she walks alone down that road both times. At the end, Joseph Cotton, who has fallen in love with her, waits up the road a ways, hoping she will acknowledge him. But the camera holds on her a long time as she walks past him without a glance. It has been a film about a war-weary world's cynicism and betrayal and about Cotton's American kind of unworldliness. His disappointment suggests a consequence of the American simpleminded idealism.

The setting's atmosphere and staging are acutely apropos. The long road, deserted save for our characters, its strong, three-dimensional visual dynamic leading toward a nonspecific distance, the bare and brutally topped trees without the softening of leaves all leave us with a resonant sense of the story.

Linkage: The Editorial Rationale ■■■■

Both the "look" and motion within the frame suggest a continuum. The look implies the next image as something looked at in the current shot. Motion in one direction suggests a continuation of that motion's direction in the next image. The mind connects successive images and tries to diagnose meaning. When the same image is flashed on the screen in different positions within successive frames, the innocent eye perceives the image as having moved from the first position to the next. This suggestion of apparent motion in Gestalt psychology is labeled the "phi" effect. The phi effect is the very basis for the illusion of motion we experience as a movie. Motion pictures are created by a succession of still images flashed on a screen at a speed of at least 16 per second. (At less than 16 per second, motion is still suggested, but not smoothly enough to allow the viewer to lose sight of distinct still images altogether.) For the innocent eye, motion is *always* present in the cut between two images. The eye must "jump" between the differences in configuration between shots. This jump, which connects to the viewer viscerally in the process of kinesthesis, can be utilized to powerful effect.

Assume a situation in which the filmmaker wishes to show the reactions of a large group of onlookers responding to an event that they all witness. He can include the event and the group in one image or, after the event occurs, cut to a separate angle of the onlooker group. Cutting to the group separate from the event causes a short lag of time between event and response, but convention accepts this as virtually the same instant. However, the images of response cited thus far allow only for a wide angle, where the reactions of individuals are submerged in the group's. If the filmmaker wishes to single out and emphasize individual reactions, perhaps to mount them into a crescendo, he can choose to cut to a quick series of individual shots. But, in what is a common mistake, *individual closeups of roughly the same size are often shown in the same positions within successive frames.* The jump between images is, therefore, de-emphasized and, to the innocent eye, the desired distinctions of separate individuals are blurred. The effect is a softening of the cut or a suggestion of the transformation of one individual into the next. This transformation may in another instance be desired, as in the special effect called "morphing," but in this case, where the separate responses of different individuals are sought, it is best to emphasize differing configurations between cuts and not let the same positioning diminish the effect.

It might be worth noting that differing configurations of like things make for a pleasurable effect even when the images are not directly joined. Early in the Orson Welles film *The Magnificent Ambersons*, the townspeople are used as a form of Greek chorus—on-camera

commentators—commenting on the status of the Ambersons, the town's leading citizens, and the arrogance of the youngest Amberson, George, the boy whose life we will follow into manhood. George is to become everyone's nemesis in the film. Welles fashioned a number of strikingly composed small group shots of the townspeople, all differently configured, and placed them at intervals throughout the beginning scenes. Even though they are not directly juxtaposed, the viewer holds the images in his memory, and there is aesthetic satisfaction achieved by the sharp delineations of the differing compositions.

The filmmaker should be aware that the photographic image on the flat screen has a limited life. Vorkapich estimated that a static shot has a lifespan of no more than ten seconds. A related fact is that returning to the same shot after once cutting away seems to subtract from the energy level of that shot. There is a sense of "having been there before"—the screen somehow goes dead. It is a virtue of good screen technique, therefore, to constantly refresh or revitalize the visual experience by the presentation of new imagery. Making a change in configuration, as in the examples cited in the Welles film, adds freshness and vitality.

Even with the common technique in which the camera cuts back and forth between two people talking to each other, the repetition of the same angles becomes visually boring. The more visually oriented directors avoid this trap as best they can by getting their characters to move frequently during dialogue interchanges. But a moving shot limits the changes that can be made in editing and can rarely be intercut smoothly.

In the editing process, unwanted variations in actor performance may be discovered or sections of dialogue may be deemed desirable to drop. For whatever reason, the order of cuts envisioned on the shooting stage may be deemed in need of change. The director must try to anticipate this possibility while filming by providing a variety of different angles of the same sequence to afford the editor a variety of choices. The exact order of sequence ultimately found to play best may not have been anticipated, but, with properly diverse coverage, its discovery is possible.

The jump to a different visual configuration clearly is the result of each cutting decision. This jump is particularly important whenever images of like content are joined in a series. Assume that a progression of forest landscapes are establishing a geographic area. The very fact that the images have similar content would tend to make them look alike and, therefore, make attempting to find distinctly different configurations more important. However, when the change of image happens between cuts, we would desire no confusion to exist even momentarily in an audience's mind.

Linkage: The Editorial Rationale

At times, the linking of images of *different* content can make the choice of *similar* configurations the better choice. I recall the opening shot of *One Flew Over the Cuckoo's Nest*. From a distant view, a camera pans slowly with a bus traveling on a road below a mountain range. The next shot, which comes after a dissolve, is a slow camera pan along figures sleeping in a hospital ward. Despite the difference in distance between mountains and sleeping bodies, on the two-dimensional screen's surface there is a pleasing match of configurations (undoubtedly accidental)—the tops of bodies and the row of mountain tops make nearly similar outlines in the same place on the screen. Here the content of the two shots is totally different, but suggested the possibility of a subtle and expressive joining—a kind of visual metaphor. Unfortunately, the pans in the two shots move in opposite directions, which to a degree inhibits the visual fluidity.

Cuts from one shot to another work as accents because there is a shift of eye motion between images. Accents are valuable ways to establish rhythms, pace, and a point of emphasis. A bad cut—often misnamed a jump cut in common editing-room parlance—occurs when two images of the same subject are juxtaposed and the jump is too slight to be certain. A good cut can be either imperceptible during action or transformation sequences, or very clearly and unambiguously underlining a definite change of shot—whichever is desired. When an action is cut in midstream, it is desirable to make a strong size change between the joining images. Otherwise the cut may have the uncomfortable effect of being only slightly perceptible—a bad cut. In the bad cut, film technique draws attention to itself and away from the film's content.

Most often, filmmakers desire to make a cut appear seamless. Whenever possible, if an incoming scene contains movement, the cut to it should be made at an early point of that incoming movement to instantly engage the innocent eye's preference for movement and give the eye time to get used to the movement. It is important to pick up the incoming movement so that it can continue long enough to register. If it is a short blip, it is another form of bad cut, attracting the eye but lasting only long enough to thwart the eye's anticipation and create a degree of confusion.

Cutting on movement creates a smooth slipping from one scene into another. It has the nature of the sleight of hand the magician uses to divert the eye for his tricks. The changes of scene have an effortless, self-propelling quality that is not unlike the images in a dream. Images replace one another without our awareness. This dream-like effect will be noted again in the comparison of linear and non-linear film structures.

Overlapping Cuts ▬▬▬▬▬▬▬▬

When cutting on continuous action, traditional technique suggests overlapping the action slightly, two or three frames—a fraction of a second—between cuts to allow the eye to adjust to the new scene. An extended overlapping was sometimes deliberately practiced by early Russian filmmakers and by Vorkapich. It is not a totally realistic experience, but adds a pleasurable form of visual syncopation through its kinetic effect on the viewer. When I first witnessed the extreme overlap—the rising bridge in Eisenstein's *Potemkin*—I thought it was unique to film, but later discovered it also to be a form of motion employed in the dance. An example in classical ballet is in the venerable Dying Swan's demise in *Les Sylphides*. The dancer/swan is shot by an arrow and then begins a slow collapse in subsiding waves. The body descends, returns part way, descends farther, comes back again not so far, and so on. This overlapping wave effect in dance or film is similar to musical syncopation and creates a strong and pleasurable visceral echo in an audience.

In Vorkapich's first cut of his filming of the storming of the English stronghold by Joan of Arc's forces, the French bring scores of ladders to lay against the walls of the enemy fortress. The English succeed in pushing many of the ladders, full of climbing Frenchmen, backward to the ground below. Vorky (as Vorkapich was affectionately called) shot and edited these falling ladders with lots of overlap, intensifying the French troops' terrifying loss of control at that moment and emphasizing by quick double beats the impact of French heads striking the ground. However, this psychologically enhanced edit was considered unrealistic, so it was recut by the producers—the overlaps eliminated—and never seen by theater audiences. Slavko, who had created enough battle scenes for film to be made an honorary general, was neither surprised nor dismayed. Like any realistic, battle-hardened veteran, he was resigned to winning some, losing some.

As mentioned earlier, the jump effect creates a visceral response. Rapid cutting intensifies this response. During rapid cutting, an acceleration in viewer pulse rate has been measured. The frenetic music-video style aims to create heightened visceral excitement. Unfortunately, in nearly all music videos, the duration of the accents or beats remain mechanically uniform and can be deemed monotonous. Since the rock music it accompanies is usually defined by an unvarying beat, there often is little or no rhythmic variety in the cutting of the video. In contrast, Vorkapich's montage sequences offer rhythmic variety even though the cutting is often rapid. "Montage" is often considered synonymous with "rapid cuts," and a variation in the rhythm of accents adds more interest, just as it does with music.

Rapid cutting will not excuse a badly planned sequencing of visuals, but, in addition to creating a pulse-changing excitement, it can provide a subtler, more artistically enriched experience. We have discussed the "limited life expectancy" of the photographic image—its information being rapidly assimilated by an audience, leaving it barren of further interest. The rapid cutting of shots leaves no image on the screen long enough for this visual exhaustion to be reached. However, it is important for the filmmaker to plan his sequencing so that the *necessary* information is transmitted unambiguously. To this end, in some cases, the filmmaker may employ a rapid-cut sequence that deliberately juxtaposes images of the same subject, albeit shot at different sizes or angles.

John Hoffman is remembered primarily for his brilliant montage of rapid cutting in the Earthquake sequence he also directed in the feature *San Francisco.* (See stills from this montage on pages 47-53.) The oft-quoted line "The devil is in the details" most fittingly describes the movie's rush of images that indelibly imprint themselves on the mind, even though they appear on screen for only a few seconds: the chandelier starting to swing, shaking wine glasses on the table, horror-struck faces looking upward, the collapsing state-capitol tower, the crash of an interior balcony, toppling walls of brick, a piano hurtling through a window, swaying lamp posts, a huge Greek god of heavy stone leaning away from its place on the corner of a building, teetering, then falling to crush a wooden wagon to splinters, one of its wheels breaking loose.

The destructive phase of the vivid Earthquake sequence ends with a cluster of shots of the wagon wheel. As it separates, spins, wobbles, and topples, *cuts overlap before they reach a position of complete rest*. After the furious pace of the cuts that precede it, the wheel spins itself out kinesthetically and metaphorically, bringing the viewer down from an adrenaline high—a wonderful image to demonstrate the violent energies of the earthquake spending themselves out.

Because this little sequence has a number of cuts of the wagon , it is imprinted in the audience's mind, even though the cuts are almost subliminal in their speed. Many rapidly cut sequences in films lose this clarity even as they achieve a level of excitement. This occurs even in the often brilliantly cut sequences of martial arts fighting in the Chinese film *Crouching Tiger, Hidden Dragon*—where the action is too fast, literally, to be seen.

Several inadvertent events in my student days taught me some unexpected ways that the jump effect could intensify actions. In one instance, two individuals collide rather violently while walking toward each other. I intended that there be a cut at the moment of collision and shot angles of the impact at two different sizes. Through some inadvertence, the filmed second shot occupied the extreme edge of the frame while the first collision occurred in mid-frame. The jump in the cut therefore carried the colliding bodies suddenly from center to frame edge, but as an unintended consequence intensified the effect of the collision.

In another instance, three colleagues and I made a film, *The Earth Sings*, in which a farm irrigation sequence began with different kinds of water sprays following one on the other. As was the agreement among us, we each took turns at making our own cut versions. In the course of frequent re-cutting, however, frames at each film splice were lost. To keep the film the same length, black frames were spliced in between the cuts. When the film was completed and a brand new print struck from the cut negative, the black frames were eliminated. My colleagues and I were stunned to find the sequence considerably weakened by losing the subliminal black frame "kicks" that had existed in the workprint.

It is important to be aware that "kicks" or accents always occur when different images are joined. When a geographic area is established with static images, the onscreen duration of those images creates a rhythm or pace, visual beats comparable to the sound beats in music. This potential for creating accents is a valuable advantage for joining static images rather than rushing too readily to use the simpler pan. It also helps guard against the filmmaker's typical fascination for creating the time-consuming moving camera shot.

ACCENTUATING OR DIMINISHING
THE VISCERAL EFFECT OF A CUT

Similar and different configurations between cuts

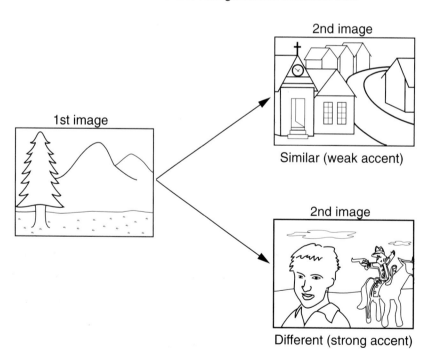

1st image

2nd image

Similar (weak accent)

2nd image

Different (strong accent)

No Cuts at All? ■■■■■■■■■■■■■

Alfred Hitchcock made a film that appeared to be in one continuous take, *Rope*. Actually, *Rope* contained *several* cuts, which were made necessary by the limited amount of film that could be contained in the camera's magazine. These edit points were prepared for by stopping the camera at moments/images where the least obtrusive cuts could be made. When projected, *Rope* seemed seamless, at least to the unprofessional eye.

Rope is not one of Hitchcock's strong films. Why the director who had made such effective use of editing in his work chose to make the film this way I am not aware, except, perhaps, to prove that he could do it or to see what the actors might be able to achieve with single uninterrupted performances, as in theatre or live television. On the other hand, the extended stage available to conventional films had to be sacrificed, and I saw no distinctive rise in the quality of the acting as compared to other Hitchcock films.

The small handheld cameras of the digital era allow for capabilities not available to Hitchcock. *Timecode*, by director Mike Figgis (noted for *Leaving Las Vegas*), is a digital foray into a four-camera, true single-take movie. In addition, each of the four camera angles is continuously presented on a screen divided into four quadrants, the audience choosing to watch where it will, nudged somewhat by the director's control of the sound levels of the scenes he deemed more or less important. It is a challenging, and at times an involving, experiment from which I believe much can be learned. It is an ensemble piece, an orchestrated mélange of personal vignettes in a physical environment directly inside and outside of a ground-floor office complex. The handheld cameras are fluid and steady, the lighting entirely from natural sources (significant advantages of the electronic medium: small cameras and great sensitivity to light). In the course of two weeks, sixteen start-to-finish takes of the movie were recorded. One was chosen, and the picture was released uncut.

I do not intend to discuss the film's story, though it is tempting to do so. Of significant note, however, is that Figgis created a story outline and the actors improvised their dialogue—a technique I will discuss later in the book. My concern here is with the way his overall technique lent itself to effective expression.

On the positive side, the fact that a large ensemble of players performed the complete picture—start to finish—sixteen times, saw each and every take after it was filmed (another capability presented by the electronic medium), and had to call on their own resources to improvise probably did produce a higher level of consistent and convincing acting performances than there might have been otherwise. In *Timecode*, this breathes life into a slack story that sometimes needs all the help it can get. The versatility of the handheld camera allowed the actors to move freely, without having to be overly concerned about camera position, bringing about a fluid, non-constricted sense of a realistic environment.

Less effective, and even unnecessary, was the four-image screen. Most of the scenes away from the main action were only occasionally interesting and detracted rather than added to the film's focus and intensity. I felt it a kind of visual noise. In and of itself, the reduction of screen size to one fourth of normal reduces the power of the image. The larger-than-life size of the movie screen in a darkened theater has always added to the movies' power to enthrall. The key scenes could have been enlarged to full size to involve the audience more intensely with perhaps the use of multiple screens when the story events they depict play as some kind of counterpoint. Writers have presented scenes within a single frame that for brief periods play at least two storylines simultaneously—usually representing the different mental places characters may inhabit even while they converse with one another. It adds a messiness that simulates real life, but in a controlled way. As far as I am concerned, Figgis has not proved any value in simultaneous screens, and his absolute rule that there be no editing is unfortunate and needlessly limiting.

Two simultaneous and separate frames work at the point in *Timecode* when a jealousy-obsessed lesbian who has planted a microphone in her lover's purse is shown in one frame, listening in agony to the orgasmic sounds of a sexual coupling between her lover and a man, who are shown simultaneously in another frame. But this is only a new wrinkle to an old convention—the secret witness overhearing what is not meant for the witness' ears. I cannot be sure if the device of two different frames adds anything to the conventional edited format of cutting back and forth between the two scenes. In the old-fashioned cross-cutting, the editor has the choice of staying longer on one scene or another. Once the sexual intrigue has begun, for example, it might be more effective to stay with the jealous lover and hear only the same sounds she hears, thus leaving more to the imagination.

What *Timecode* suggests is that there are virtues to be found in the actor being able to act non-stop—beginning to end, in improvisation—and in the fluidity of the handheld camera.

The Potential of Editing:
"The Screen Will Tell"

A film editor could say that the perfect film will be made only when someone creates a magical film bin in which the shot you need will always be found hanging on a pin. Film bins have given way to digital databanks, but the editor's dream of exactly the right shot when needed is still never satisfied. An ironic comment on an editor's mindset is that he nearly always faults the director for letting him down (even when he, himself, is that director). Such is the editorial process, a stage where needs that can never be fully foreseen or met are created. But it is where unexpected discovery and almost magical creation also occur.

Editing can be a magical time because, unlike the scripting or the directing, this is when the actual recorded images and sounds are joined. The film is no longer a creature of intentions and scripted words on paper but physical fact, having its own independent life. The juxtaposition of the filmed images in the edit always generates new possibilities.

"The screen will tell" is, indeed, the accepted truth of a moviemaker's life. As the movie is assembled, new perspectives emerge, intentions are judged by their results. Painful discoveries can come to light: Scenes that demanded unusual, difficult effort and sometimes great financial cost may be nonetheless found to be deficient, and may even need to be discarded. But during editing a way might also be discovered for the movie to be much improved with elements or nuances added in ways that were never anticipated.

The moviemaker must find the honesty in himself to recognize whatever it is the screen tells him—which is not as easy as it may sound. He may have been so fiercely committed to getting a scene "right" that he cannot recognize when the result does not measure up to his intentions. Deciding that a sequence may be lacking, even if that sequence contains the work of a star who cost a fortune to secure, is a hard truth to face. It can force the moviemaker to feel like a father who must condemn his own child.

A director must see with a director's eye as well as with a cinematographer's and an editor's eyes. On the movie set, assistants (the script supervisor, perhaps the editor, the cinematographer, all of whom have a developed movie sense) can help the director's decision process, and, of course, the script already contains the film's structure. But an editor's eye recognizes the "magic bin" as the ideal, so a director must strive to provide as many options for the editing process as can be conjured up, and to try his best to prepare for what *cannot be foreseen*.

Options are created by the coverage of a scene from many different camera angles. Budget and time are constraints on this coverage, so a director must learn to choose what is most likely to be of value. An extra closeup can allow for a helpful point of emphasis or to cover a deleted section of the dialogue. An extra wide-angle shot can be available to break intensity by offering space and breathing room within a scene.

Overly generous coverage can also be abused by a director who has a very weak conception of a scene's structure and shoots every angle possible for a later choice to be made in editing. This *over* coverage, because it is without plan, tends to become formulaic and mechanical: wide-angle, two-shot, single, single—again and again. It also lacks the originality and fire a director can provide from his special vision. *Under* coverage is perpetrated by directors who want to protect their conception of a scene by providing *only* the necessary footage for their favored structure. (This is a process called *cutting in the camera*.) This limits the editing to one choice and cuts off the creative process before editing can complete it.

The ideal solution is for the director to provide a rich and varied palette for the editing room by visualizing several structures for each scene, as well as providing the odd extra shots, such as closeups for possible cutaways.

Other preparations for the *unforeseeable* rely on the director's *discoveries* while film-ing. One simple example occurred while I was filming a documentary about the controver-sial crime figure Caryll Chessman. The actual courtroom where his trial took place was my setting. Journalist Quentin Reynolds was present as the host and stood below the judge's bench. J. Miller Levy, who had prosecuted the case, stood where he actually had stood during the trial, and a woman juror spoke from the very seat she had occupied in the jury box. I was struck by the subtle suggestion of drama in the atmosphere of the bare court-room where Chessman and so many others had heard their fates decided. I chose to make use of this in a simple way. I either panned to these people from a significant spot, such as the chair Chessman sat in, before they spoke, or I panned to a significant spot after they had finished their comments. These were hardly extraordinary decisions, but my anticipation of *unforeseen possibilities* in the later edit proved prescient.

These "significant spots" became either moments when the narration prepares the way for an on-camera speaker or when musical beats (called "stingers") underline a point after the speaker has had his say.

Intellectual Content ▬▬▬▬▬▬

Around 1917, both the film medium's rise to importance and the Russian Communist Revolution were exciting the theorists of their day. Soviet director Sergei Eisenstein wrote from a Marxian perspective that montage (used in the sense only of the mounting of motion picture images in sequence) always expressed conflict. According to Marxist theory, based on Hegel's concept of the dialectic process, when two opposing or conflicting forces (the thesis and antithesis) meet, a new meaning—or synthesis—is created. While there is some truth in Eisenstein's statement, Vorkapich was quick to point out that not all montage was conflict—some elements could be deemed reinforcing or collaborative.

When the motion picture was in its early historical stages, theories about the new medium's nature and significance were popular with intellectuals. Things have settled down and, perhaps unfortunately, there is less intellectual excitement in general about film form today. (During Vorkapich's lifetime, the stimulus and intellectual rigor of his lectures rekindled some of the excitement of film's early days.) Today there are nebulous standards. Critics are highly inconsistent. Commercial values—popularity contests—mingle with serious criticism, and little if any distinction exists between photo-dramatic and filmic qualities.

From the start, however, some film-theory camps had a tendency to overvalue the degree of intellectual complexity possible with pure images. This has persisted. The problem derives from the unrefined nature of the photographed image. Most images contain a great range of elements of differing significance. To isolate any single idea from the matrix requires an arbitrary, unconscious choice by the viewer and usually reflects his predispositions or prejudices. Other than the photographing of a verbal message—a sign, a newspaper heading, etc.—a photographed image can imply any number of meanings.

A critic's commentaries are often overblown with the rhetoric of his presumptions. One director whom I often find unusually obscure, the Italian Michelangelo Antonioni, was for a time the darling of these critics. Much significance was claimed for images of smokestacks in his film *Red Desert.* I felt the context did not warrant the interpretation, and honestly forget what it was claimed the smokestacks represented. However, t I have indulged in some likely possibilities: From a Freudian perspective, Antonioni's smokestacks might be construed as phallic symbols, representing either sexual power or sexual abuse; from a Marxian point of view, they might be thought to symbolize a skyward thrust of man's indomitable energy, the success of State planning; or from an artist's or environmentalist's position, the same smokestacks might signify the poisoning of the land, the obscuring of beautiful blue sky by billowing gray smoke, a blotting out of poetic feeling. Take your pick. But the camera lens is a neutral recording device without capacity for interpretation. Whatever was meant, I would have to learn in some other way than by merely seeing smokestacks. I would need assistance from words in narration or dialogue. If the director could somehow pinpoint his lens to reveal only what was relevant to his intellectual concept, he might suggest at least a particle of his intellectual meaning. To directly and specifically communicate a complex idea, he would need to photograph a printed page.

I contend that specific intellectual content of any degree of complexity is not in the province of a film's imagery, but must be left to the verbal vehicles of narration and dialogue. Images can suffice only for generalizations. For example: A single shot of a few birds or several shots of birds may signify an idea of birds, but when shots of birds taking off from the ground are joined with scenes of birds flying, then juxtaposed with airplanes and perhaps flying balloons, we may infer a concept of flight.

Considerable time must be taken with pictures to achieve what written language can produce in seconds. The visual progression of birds into flight does *contain a poetic quality*, which is, perhaps, the very result of its *lack* of specificity. Since the human mindinherently attempts to fashion meaning, an audience is brought into imaginative participation (empathy) with a scene by searching for its ideas. With the introduction of sound, words became available to express concrete ideas, and the use of imagery was reduced to a more literal recording of performance. An exterior shot of a house within which action was taking place simply announced, sign-like, that this was a type of house. Snow falling announced, sign-like, that this was winter. The actors and the photoplay with sound then conveyed all other ideas of greater complexity, and with the images advanced the action.

Narration and Film

Narration and what is termed the "voice-over" (comments by an off-screen character) are frequently a part of documentary films and television commercials and, now and again, are inserted into dramas. In the budget-constrained documentaries that appear on cable television, the narration is usually continuous (what is referred to as "wall-to-wall"). In such a case, the imagery is comparable to slides illustrating a lecture. I have nothing against this form of information-giving. If the text has the facts and is interesting, it suffices to do its job. (This common form of documentary should not be compared, however, to the documentaries that have explored and exploited the moviemaking form: from the earliest films of Robert Flaherty, such as *Nanook of the North* and *Man of Aram*, to the Willard Van Dyck and Pare Lorentz collaborations *The Plough That Broke the Plains* and *The River* to the cinéma vérité works of Frederick Wiseman, such as *Titicut Follies* and *Hospital*, where the image is dominant and narration is entirely absent.)

A good narration must take into account not only the demands of language and subject matter, but the limits of length prescribed by a cut film. It must be planned to allow moments of respite from a continuous drone of words. In a pattern called "checkerboarding," periods of narration frequently alternate with periods in which the visuals stand alone.

Words are a concentrated form of expression that greatly alter and at times suppress the qualities pure imagery can create. Remember, the art of film is essentially one of images and motion, not of the spoken word, which can be said to best suit radio drama, poetry readings, rap singing, and speechmaking. Sentences are structured forms that take a period of time to complete, just as a series of connected scenes does in a film. This unfurling of word and picture can be made to fit together in a way that particularly suits the relationship of the two elements.

With all its constraints—the narration's need to conform to film length, the match of word and image, the synchronization between the order of the film's images and verbal syntax, etc.—good film writing is something like trying to perform a ballet in a closet.

A Simple Demonstration of Synchronizing Word and Picture

IMAGE	NARRATION
Series of scenes:	
Man climbs difficult mountain.	*Is man's achievement any less . . .*
Man's head appears over top	
edge of mountain.	
Shot widens to include what he sees.	
A couple sitting comfortably	
on a bench at top of mountain.	
They watch sunset.	*if someone else got there first?*

Good narration does not describe the picture it accompanies, but adds an intellectual or emotional content that is the pure province of words.

Anyone who has written film narration has been confronted by how short a strip of film becomes when the narrator tries to fit in his words. Narration writing calls for continual paring of essentials until there is an absolute economy of expression, but that does not mean that the writing cannot be beautiful, or that the words cannot become music. As prime examples, I suggest viewing the New Deal-era documentaries *The Plough That Broke the Plains* and *The River. The River* won the Best Documentary prize at the 1938 Venice Film Festival, and Pare Lorentz's Walt Whitman-like narration in it was nominated for a Pulitzer Prize in poetry.

Poetry: Film and Word

Meshing written poetry and film is an interesting challenge. Because poetry is frequently expressed by verbal imagery, the filmmaker is sometimes confused as to the way it can be synchronized with film. Poetry's imagery, it must be remembered, is based on the metaphoric resonance found in verbal language and is not necessarily a literal depiction of a visual reality. Assume one is fashioning a film—a cinematographic structure—that will play in parallel to the famous opening lines of Dylan Thomas's poem:

Do not go gentle into that good night,
Old age should burn and rave at close of day;
Rage, rage against the dying of the light.

The words "good night," their meaning reemphasized as "close of day" and "dying of the light," are not images that one can photograph so that, by themselves, they impart the poet's intended meaning. The words impart a somber grandeur; they are metaphors for death.

"The light" of the poem refers to the light of life, again not automatically implied by a specific image.

How can we construct such a film? What I have seen attempted are banal pictorials that repeat in a tepid way the imagery of the words. One has the challenge of constructing a parallel film using the essential nature of the film form to achieve a poetic character that *fits* the poem's words. In this case, the poem itself becomes the film's narration.

Remember that the Dylan Thomas lines are complete, while my little script, which follows, is only an outline for a film still to be realized. With full apology to any who may deem this effort an offense to Dylan Thomas's spirit, I offer the following attempt.

PICTURE	NARRATION
A man's head lies still and prone in profile on a pillow. People move alongside the bed, but are unclear, as if diffused by a veil. The SOUND is muted and undecipherable, a murmur of hushed voices. Close on the prone head of an old man. He turns sharply as if in a spasm of resistance. He faces toward the camera, his eyes wide, fearful, his face pale and sweating. Persons on both sides of the man's bed bring up the blanket to cover his face. Several overlapping angles of the blanket moving to cover him.	
The man, MUTE, but eyes wide, is lowered into a coffin. The coffin lid is slid over the top, upward from the bottom, matching the movement of the covering blanket.	

PICTURE (continued)	**NARRATION (continued)**
A shadow of the lid slides up over the man's terrified face. Suddenly— still in the bed, the prone man arches his back in spasm and lets out an anguishing cry.	
The CRY LINGERS over a group of pallbearers (seen in silhouette) carrying the coffin on their shoulders. They walk on the rim of a hill. The horizon is still bright, but the sky is darker toward the top of the frame. The sound of the pallbearer's footsteps crunch the earth. (The image is more stylized than real.) The moon in the dark sky. Clouds begin to move across its face.	*Do not go gentle into that good night,* *Old age should burn and rave at close of day;* *Rage, rage against the dying . . .* *of the light.*
The man's face writhes, contorts, cries out. It merges slowly with the full moon as	(the sound of his cry)
shadows move across the doubled image. The moon disappears, leaving man's face in the clear. He arches his neck in a final spasm	

PICTURE (continued)	**NARRATION (continued)**

PICTURE (continued)

of surrender, then dies, his
head falling back abruptly.
The cloud covers the moon.
A shadow covers the man and
fades into total black.
In the black, the crunch of
footsteps continues.
The man's voice faintly cries out.
The sound of footsteps
die away.

NARRATION (continued)

(repeated faintly)
Rage, rage against the dying of the light.

The Hidden Film

The great Danish film director and essayist Carl Dreyer referred to a "third dimension of time" in film. He was not speaking of a visual third dimension, but of what others have called the "hidden film," which is said to run parallel with the one on the screen. It is the subjective narrative, the emotional play of expectations generated within the audience. It is a living film of the imagination kindled by the film on the screen—by its story, its actors' performances, its director's hand, and the evocative quality of its images.

The Film Story ▬▬▬▬▬▬▬▬▬▬

When I describe a scene, I capture it with the moving eye of the cine-camera rather than the photographer's eye—which leaves it frozen. —Graham Greene

. . . the motion picture is not a transplanted literary or dramatic art . . . in its essential nature, it is much closer to music, the sense that the finest effects can be independent of precise meaning, that its transitions can be more eloquent than its hi-lit scenes, and its dissolves and camera movements . . . are often more effective than its plots. —Raymond Chandler

This chapter is not intended to be about writing a screenplay, except for those points of nexus between the written word and the visual image or, in a larger sense, where the story cannot be separated from the filmic experience. Story is, of course, a very vital part of what we have called the "hidden film." Its function is to suggest the elements that, when transformed into film, will engage the empathetic imagination of the viewer. The story must outline a path that will hold the viewer's interest and create emotion, but, at the same time, it must be designed to lend itself to filmic interpretation. The story on paper is not the film; the projected film is not the words on paper. The very act of first conceiving a film on paper can be questioned, since it sets up a form that tends to be most immediately responsive to the written word. Even when the director is the writer and fashions a movie script, he will feel the tugs of the literary form and can be pulled away from an expression that, rather than being an adjunct to his filmmaking, is an entity all to itself. This problem can grow when the script has to be judged by others who are not filmmakers, but executives used to reading scripts and comparing one reading experience to another.

Savvy screenwriters are known to prepare themselves for this trial by writing scripts designed to "make a good read," cutting down on visual description, knowing they will be judged by the voltage in their peppy dialogue. (Some executives confess to only reading the dialogue when scanning a script.) What happens then to the visual essence—the image and movement partnership we have been talking about, to Graham Greene's "moving eye of the cine-camera"? That moving eye may have been pre-censored, never put into the script, or thrown out with the scene descriptions.

For a long time, I have been interested in the possibility of bridging the gap between the written word and film, finding a more flexible interface between the writing and the filmmaking process. I've hoped that the writer could break out of his sedentary and sequestered office and mesh his efforts with a film in progress. In 1970, I attempted to mount a production that would accomplish this. At that time, many young people in Europe were setting out on spiritual quests or seeking plentiful supplies of cheap hashish by journeying from points in Europe to India and Nepal, where they believed enlightenment beckoned. These migrations were colorful and dramatic: contrasting naive idealism with the rascality of drug-dealing and the rampant smuggling of art objects with serious threats of running afoul of authorities and possible incarceration in primitive prisons or of a worse end— wasted and penniless in countries with millions of other mouths contesting for any morsel of food. This all took place on a journey that took the camera through a wonderfully varying landscape of countries and cultures.

My plan was to write an outline story with someone who had taken such a trek and assemble a cast that mixed actual trekkers and actors of similar age and nature. We would then begin the actual journey with a small film crew and feel free to improvise the dialogue and to deviate from the outline's plot if events were suggested by the real experience or actually happened on the way. I felt that the outline would be enough to keep us on course for maintaining a coherent storyline.

I wrote the outline with a delightful guy, Though poor, he happened to be an Irish Lord and a bit of a rogue who "had been there and done that" as far as much of what I cited above was concerned.

Though the budget for the film was very modest, in the end, our studio backing refused to sanction a production based just on an outline. Winter was getting close and we had to delay until the following year while trying to find another financing source. Unfortunately, by the next summer, such migrations were a thing of the past and the project had to be abandoned.

Writing a Filmic Outline

Vorkapich made two short films to music that were wonderful in their photography and extraordinary in their editing. They were based on Wagner's *Forest Murmurs* (from the opera *Siegfried*) and Mendelssohn's *Fingal's Cave* overture.

Many films had been made to accompany previously composed music. Nearly all of these simply ran a series of pretty pictures alongside music with only the barest connection between the two elements. What Vorkapich did was to create a vital correspondence between them. Rhythms and movements mesh, visual intensity merges with musical emotion, visualized breathing room accompanies moments of respite. The connections between image and music are subtle and appear as if unplanned. None of this should be confused with the apish, mechanical, and obvious style known as "Mickey Mousing," which, in the style of comic animated cartoons, slavishly underlines and amplifies every on-screen action with a sound-effect-like bit of music.

An interesting exercise is to test different pieces of music joined to the same strip of film. Some pieces never mesh, but other—quite different—selections may engender very new ways of seeing the same filmed material. It is remarkable to discover the range of qualities different music pieces can bring—one's very perception of the movie images changes. If this has happened with a film we have made ourselves, contemplate, with full humility, what exactly "joins" film and music in this instance so that it creates an effect not planned nor desired and how subtly it may enhance or detract from the film that we thought we made. Sometimes the effect is not necessarily good or bad, but just different, perhaps revealing unanticipated elements imbedded in our visualization. Certainly the fusion of these two elements reinforces Raymond Chandler's claim about similarities in the two art forms. I think, at the very least, it may offer valuable insights into selecting appropriate music.

Vorky suggested writing a visual scrip— that is, a verbal description of just a film's intended visual elements—as a working guide rather than a hard and fast design, in which one attempts to engender one's words with the desired emotions. This visual script (an outline, really) could then serve as an emotional guide as well as a visual one. He showed us such a script he wrote for a short music film he wanted to make to Sibelius's *The Swan of Tuonela*.

Here is a script excerpt, along with Vorkapich's own statement of premise.

THE SWAN OF TUONELA, a Film Treatment by Slavko Vorkapich.

In this briefly outlined filmic interpretation of Jan Sibelius's great tone poem, an attempt has been made to expand the local Finnish legend into a more universal theme of the periodic dying in Nature before the onset of winter. In the Finnish myth, the disembodied souls of humans are led by the sacred swan to the underground caverns of Tuonela, the Inferno of Finnish mythology.

THE SWAN OF TUONELA

A drowsy, motionless bird on a bare branch.
Gloomy clouds floating over barren trees.
Mirrored in vast northern lake,
The pale reflection
Of a sinking sun
Where the mythical swan is born.
Slowly the transparent vision of the sacred bird
Grows until it almost covers
The expanse of lake, sky, and screen.
With a majestic turn of its supple neck,
The Swan's head surveys
Its melancholy domain.

Sees the drooping reeds.
The trembling leaves.
The wilting flower.
The brooding bird on the branch.

The Swan spreads its enormous wings:
Monumental, eerie, deliberate, and slow
. . . while, tugged by an icy breeze,
A dead leaf lets go
And twirling down
Floats slowly to the ground.

Within the heart of the dead leaf
A blurred phantom image stirs.
Awakening, it grows clear:
In human form, the soul of the leaf
Arises and soars.

From a tiny wilted flower
The translucent image of its soul
The tender shape of a child
Disengages itself to follow.

Again, the arc of the great Swan's wings
Signal the journey
And stir the wind.

A dead branch breaks and falls
Down from a barren tree:
And the spectral image of an aged man
Is carried by the gusts
Up from the withered branch.

The carpet of dry leaves jostle in the wind,
A rustle of phantom wings stir
The lifeless body of a bird
And now its spirit awakens
And joins a phantom flock.

The Swan turns, and like the mother
Followed by her brood, leads the spectral cortege.

The still reflection of the snow-capped mountains
Quiver in the rolling wake.
A gentle wash laps the shore
And receding carries off
The company of fallen leaves.

Moved by the rolling ripples,
The overhanging willow branches Sway.
As we glide past gloomy crags
Past
Leafless trees and lonely shores
Past
The tormented frozen shapes of winter until,
Leaving behind the land of mortals,
The cortege passes through icy portals,
Enters the unearthly brilliance
Of the boreal light.
From the depths of the arctic night
Luminous fringes
Unfold and sway.
Curtains of eerie radiance dart,
Interweaving in cosmic play.

Superimposed Images and Metaphor

We have all been held by the interesting visual mixtures we sometimes see when we look through glass and see both the scene beyond and the reflection of ourselves or of the place where we are standing. Vorkapich used "superimposure" frequently in his montages. In modern films, this merging of images has fallen from favor, which I think is unfortunate. Superimposure can add an elusive complexity to the frame that transcends the literal aspect of photography.

I experienced two cases of accidental double exposures on film that made me aware, too, of how such combined images can add a richness of metaphor that transcends the separate images. In one instance, I was taking still pictures of a friend's wedding, and I posed the bride and groom in full formal wedding attire, smiling joyfully while standing against a simple undifferentiated background. My eye's alignment with the viewfinder was faulty—no doubt a result of the free-flowing champagne—and the snap placed the couple at the bottom of the frame. My next shot—equally alcoholic—accidentally superimposed four aged Hungarian-born grandparents, dressed in the dark suits of old-country formality, standing unsmiling in front of a gated arch—one of the men was stooped, helping to support himself with a gnarled cane. In the double-exposed image, the old people in black are seen in much larger size than the wedding couple, the partly transparent grandparents looming over the newlyweds like judgmental specters. A sense had been created that whatever their moment's joy, the young couple would be haunted by their family pasts. A striking image!

Another accidental double exposure made on 8mm film created a perhaps less specific symbolism. I was filming my family at the beach and finished with a ground-level angle of the foaming edge of waves racing up the sandy incline at the beach's edge and then sliding back. The retreating water left a full screen of glistening, flattened sand before another wave repeated the process. For reasons I cannot recall, this last beach shot was rolled back and exposed again while I filmed a bullfight in Tijuana, Mexico. Bullfighter and lunging bull were at a full-figure distance. When I looked at the processed film, I saw the bull making his furious passes at the matador's cape while ocean water rolled across the screen and receded. The sparkling wet sand added a luminance while wave and bull surged and lunged, both coordinating with the billowing cape, merging in an unexpected and beautiful way. It suggested a connection between all the movements, perhaps symbolizing nature's violent forces.

I was held by the superimposed shots and watched them again and again. Nothing in the rest of the footage—my family at the beach and of the bullfight in Tijuana—held a similar fascination.

I like to use the word "resonance" to describe something of what happened in my two double-exposure incidents. "Resonance" is used to describe supplementary vibrations in mechanical and electrical systems. In art, I use it to mean the afterglow or the aura emanating from a work of art that is greater than the sum of its parts and is a measure of its artistic quality. It is something that can never be fully explained, and contains an element of mystery that outlives the shot.

The Soberness of the Shot

The two examples of superimposure cited above overcame what Vorkapich called "the soberness of the shot." He used this phrase to describe the literal or purely recording aspect of photography. He also coined the word "mech" for the mechanical aspects of the moviemaking process as well as the literal, recording aspect of photography. He often derided an overzealous infatuation with motion picture technology as a worship "of the great god Mech" and saw the filmmaker's job as one where the mechanical and literal (purely reproductive) aspects of the medium, its "soberness," had always to be transcended.

Conrad Hall, preparing the scene from *In Cold Blood* in which actor Robert Blake, playing a murderer awaiting death as punishment for his crime, talks to a chaplain about his emotionally barren life, used lighting and physical effect to eloquent purpose to capitalize on the scene's emotion.

Blake talks while he stands next to a small cell window. It is raining. The light comes from outside and must pass through the window's glass. Droplets from the rain scroll downward over its surface. The light is distorted by the drops in a way that makes Blake's face take on the mottling effect of the descending water, a kind of melting. We can deduce the cause to be the rain, so we do not think of it as effect. It is extremely subtle, it is as if Blake's entire face is shedding tears. The emotional resonance is in perfect tune with the moment.

Maintaining a Consistent Visual Style ■

In the animated film, consistency of style is readily maintained by the images being the product of either a single artist or an agreed-upon kind of Disney-group style. Every frame of a Disney-animated film is in the same style. In the non-animated film, set design (whether using color or black-and-white film), lighting, camera angle, and costuming are all made to fit first with the overall genre of the piece: be it musical, comic, historical, action thriller, film-noir, or anything else. Subtler differences may be designed to fit a *given scene* according to its emotional content and mood. The sustained and tragic poignancy created by the raindrop distortions on Robert Blake's face (in *In Cold Blood*) would have been unsuited to a comedy scene.

The camera's sobriety, the mechanical and literal quality already mentioned, is a trap to the unwary, ready to disrupt stylistic cohesion. I recall a vivid instance in which a change in style *between shots* acutely disrupted an effective mood. In the 1950s, when cameras were first taken underwater in the hands of free-swimming divers, a fascinating new visual world was presented to viewers of film and television. I was fascinated by my first underwater view of human divers traveling through an undersea world, seemingly weightless, sharing a sense of physical freedom to move in any direction, tug at a dolphin's tail or tease an octopus. Then a scene I was watching cut suddenly to three rather prosaic characters lit by the sun in sharp contrasting tones, immobile, peering over the side of a small boat, apparently at the swimmers below. It was a visual shock. I felt physically wrenched out of my enchantment with a rarely seen world and hurled into the mundane and everyday.

I pondered what I had experienced. Accepting that the cut to the watchers in the boat had been a necessary story point, I pondered how visual shock might have been avoided. I decided that stylistic integrity could have been maintained by the way the three watchers were shot. It would have needed special effort—the angle might have been from underwater, the lens pointing up from close to the water's surface, catching the watchers' images distorted by the water's refraction and undulation, or an angle that continued the movement they were experiencing under the water might have been set up from the surface by photographing them as they moved through low-hanging branches stretching out from a large tree on the shore, for instance. The important point for the filmmaker is to be sensitive to stylistic consistency in the first place.

Sleight of Eye ▬▬▬▬▬▬▬▬▬

Vorkapich's montages with their skillful use of motion to divert the eye—by rapid cutting between scenes or by frequent changes within a shot—prevented an unvaried image from being on screen long enough for all of its visual information to be fully absorbed. He argued that it was necessary to maintain some degree of mysteriousness—some things not fully comprehended—to keep a shot alive, which is exactly what Conrad Hall does with his rainwater shot in *In Cold Blood*. The viewer grasps that the effect is created by descending droplets of rain on the glass, but the connection of the visual effect to the dramatic moment in the scene is unexpected and resonates with emotion. Hall brought the image a considerable distance from the literal record.

For Conrad Hall, overcoming the soberness of the shot is accomplished by working outward from an internalized perspective. "I take into account the director's point of view," he told me, "but I must feel a scene in my own bones. When I get ready to make a shot, I follow two guides: the director's and my internal sense of what is to be accomplished. The visual just comes to me. It includes the emotion, the characters, the story, and the scene."

The film *American Beauty*, which Conrad photographed, has a sequence in which the young male lead returns to his room, where his enraged father is waiting to accuse him of lewd behavior in the neighbor's house. "I had to decide where to put the light and where not to put the light in order to lend a suitable aura to the drama that will take place between father and son," Connie told me. "It is a choice about when to reveal the father and in what way— what kind of light and where?"

"We chose not to reveal the father as the scene begins, but let it come as a surprise. We hear his voice first, but the first time we actually see him he is barely visible, a shape sitting

in the dark—an ominous presence. Right away we know this is not going to be a nice, comfortable scene. The father's voice is harsh, accusing, and even as he gets up, he remains in silhouette. When he enters our light, he is harshly lit, cruel. The scene is totally orchestrated—lighting scheme, actor's movement, composition, and cutting design.

"It is a brutal scene that continues a chain of tragic circumstances—a dark scene. It is impossible to imagine the scene as brightly lit. It needs the dark to have its resonance."

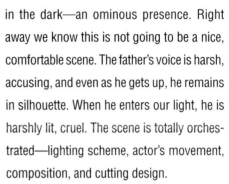

Directing the Visual ███████████████████

We see by these examples that where the camera and lights are placed and what lenses are used have a wide range of consequences. After many years of moviemaking, I was still surprised on one occasion to see how bad camera placement and flat lighting could effectively destroy a scene.

I know it is unfair to compare a student's inexperienced effort with Conrad Hall's work, but I will cite a student work here because the example underlines how dramatically visual understandin— or, in this case, the lack of it—can affect a scene. The student had written an exemplary short script based on the famous Ernest Hemingway short story "A Clean Well-Lighted Place," which I deferred to her request to direct without supervision.

The student missed a chance to take some clue from the title's mention of light. The lighting is, indeed, a particularly important aspect to the tale's telling. Perhaps overly anxious that her images should be recorded at all, she ordered lights of a single intensity placed uniformly over her sole set. The same mechanical logic guided her camera placement. Technically, her objective was successful: All the words and actions she had written were scrupulously documented. However, despite competent actors, the drama and emotion in the script were almost totally lost. The action in Hemingway's story occurs in the late hours of the evening, when one of a café's two waiters is impatient to lock up the restaurant and go home. However, the sole patron lingers at his table interminably. It is a story of loneliness and of emptiness and elicits the famous "nada"/"nothing" soliloquy, "Our nada who art in nada, nada be thy name . . ."

Instead of its undifferentiated flatness, the lighting might have suggested the lateness of the hour with shadows and darkened spaces. Indeed, the story has two references to the shadows of moving leaves cast by a tree near the restaurant terrace and the street lamp. They are described by the older waiter, who is himself a lonely soul, as a positive aspect of the nighttime café—an accent to its being brightly lit and comforting. For the "clean well-lighted place" suggested by Hemingway as a nighttime haven for the lonely, the visual details in this story of mood are all important. The camera angles might have stressed the single customer's basic loneliness in the very fact that he is a solitary figure in a nearly empty restaurant—the pauses in dialogue could have been accentuated by angles of tables and chairs without people. None of this was given any thought, so the story, which depended so much on visual elements to convey its mood, fell totally flat.

One can understand from this student's example what Conrad Hall was referring to when he said that brightly lighting the aforementioned scene in the young male's room in *American Beauty* would have destroyed its "resonance."

The province of the cinematographer is the image. As we have seen, it can be executed as mechanical reproduction or as original vision. If he is to transcend the soberness of the shot, the cinematographer will make his images poetic or beautiful or unexpected. They must fuse with the story being told. Great images extend far out from mere representation and reverberate in an audience's unconscious mind, where their effect tends to linger after the image has physically gone from view.

Light and Shadow ■■■■■■■■■■

The affect of light on a scene is usually described by its affect on color intensity. Not as much recognition is made of light's ever-present partner—shadow. (However, Hemingway recognized it as he described the shadows of the leaves cast by the street lamps in "A Clean Well-Lighted Place.") The contrasting black shadow reinforces the vividness of all that is not in shadow. It is tempting to develop this fact in a philosophical or metaphysical way, but I will confine my comments to visual aesthetics. The shadow side of individual leaves of grass is most pronounced when the sun is low in the late afternoon. Many photographers limit their exterior work to the time of the late afternoon sun, because its angle casts a dramatic dark offset to all objects: A landscape is rarely more beautiful, a face more dramatic, and the clarity of an object more defined. The dark shadow, of course, has been the place for the mysterious—a room full of shadows holds secrets; an over-lighted room, none.

I was never made more aware of this than the time I taped President Gerald Ford at Camp David. Magnetic tape had just come into use as a means of recording images for television broadcast. It was the first time I had relied on that technology, and I was not fully aware of the way its image differed from that of film. Camp David, as has been recorded many times, is strewn with winding paths through woods. I set up a shot where Betty Ford and the President walk down such a path toward the camera, then Mrs. Ford takes a different path and the camera follows the President as he walks alone for a distance. The object, of course, was to emphasize the symbol of the President as ultimately alone with the big decisions for which he is responsible.

My experience with film led me to expect a definite visual quality that would resonate poetically as the President walked away. What was actually produced was a "pretty" picture that lacked any resonant quality. When I analyzed the problem, I realized that the tape had less latitude for visual density, i.e., the range and degrees of change from pure white to pure black were only about a third of what film allowed. There was no pure black, and what would have been black shadow areas on film were presented as lightened by hues of color. With the shadows absent, the *mysterious* disappeared, the implicit became explicit, and the resonance I was striving for—a scene that showed more than just a man alone on a path, but the president alone with his unique and awesome responsibilities—was never conveyed. Shadow areas would have allowed me to imply more than the scene actually showed.

Moments ▚▚▚▚▚▚▚▚▚▚▚▚▚▚▚▚▚▚▚

The filmmaker must never lose sight of the difference between actuality and its reproduction onto film. Every dramatic scene could be analyzed as having key *moments* when the course of the story shifts dramatically: a wife learns of her husband's infidelity, a character realizes he or she is in love, a man on trial realizes his fate is sealed. On the stage, the actor makes sure the audience registers these critical points by some device of enlargement or added emphasis. In good acting, the device is subtle, perhaps not even noticed. On the screen, acting is best when downplayed. Where the camera is placed, image size, and where the cuts are made may have as much to do with the effectiveness of the moment as the performance.

In the directorial failure of the student effort I cited previously and in much of the student work I have reviewed, this glossing over the "moment" was a common error. As he prepares for shooting a scene, the director should make note of these many story peaks, not only with a view to fully understanding his story, but also as to get them onto film with clarity and emphasis.

A Moment

In the film *Witness,* directed by Peter Weir, one such key moment occurs when Harrison Ford, a New York detective recuperating from a bullet wound and hiding out from men who mean to kill him, has to make a key decision. He is being sheltered by a devout Amish farm family, and he must decide whether to follow his emotions and sexual desire and make love to a young Amish widow played by Kelly McGillis. Ford and McGillis have a growing sexual attraction, but we have become aware of how deep the cultural divide is between them and how much one or the other would have to sacrifice if they allowed their attraction to be fulfilled. McGillis's character would face being ostracized by the community in which she has lived all her life and would violate the principles she has lived by. Yet she is the one most inclined to risk all.

In more ordinary films, the decision would have been made in a dialogue scene between the two, but in *Witness*, the moment is decided without speech.

A rumble of thunder at dusk. The air is humid and still. Except for Ford and McGillis, the family has gone to bed. McGillis is alone in the kitchen and has decided to sponge herself down in the summer heat. Ford is alone outside. He is troubled and heavy with indecision. She strips off the top of her dress and begins soaping her bare upper torso. There are several angles of her, including one through the window. We are aware that Ford might also be able to see her, though we don't know if he does. McGillis is serene, neutral, but aware of the sensual atmosphere. Ford comes to the door of the kitchen and looks in. Sensing his presence, McGillis turns around. The two look at each other, McGillis frank and unashamed, Ford uncertain. Their exchange of looks lingers, neither moving. Ford, sadly, turns around and walks away. McGillis looks after him and resumes her soaping.

A "moment" has been captured.

Acting for the Camera:
A Few Tricks

The intimacy of the closeup and the literalness of the camera lens have largely determined a specific movie-acting style. The closeup, from a purely technical point of view, requires the actor to restrict his movements to keep within the limited area of the screen. The scrutiny of a full-screen closeup demands an "inner" style of acting rather than an outwardly physical one (such as stage acting) that would be exaggerated by the closeup's enlargement. In ways that defy easy analysis, the camera seems to reveal a sense of the actor's ("inner") thought processes.

Great movie actors are able to convey a thinking and feeling life that will support the requirements of any script. It is astonishing the degree to which a great actor intrigues our interest with an ever-present, if subtle, charisma. The fine actor always hints at a sub-textual content along with the action he is performing.

Director Elia Kazan, working with a young Marlon Brando in *On the Waterfront*, dealt with a scene in which Brando's character is in distress over having to reveal secrets. Kazan asked him to play the scene as if he had an intense need to urinate. The imagined physical discomfort, an intense desire to be someplace else, fit perfectly with the content of the scene and intensified Brando's performance.

Though the movie actor's conviction is generated by inner processes, these processes are revealed by outward physiological manifestations that the camera unerringly records.

These often-subtle variations in expression and body language frequently occur without the actor's conscious awareness or guidance.

Kazan could be brutal on the outside to get the actor to become brilliant on the inside. While shooting *On the Waterfront*, when attempting to elicit signs of remorse and guilt from a young actor as part of his confession to murdering Marlon Brando's pet pigeons, Kazan reportedly felt forced to use more than acting suggestions to get the young non-professional's tears to flow on cue. (Tears look the same whether compelled by the actor's imagination or a hard pinch.)

The response to seeing or hearing something shocking is difficult to *act*. Shock is a non-thinking physiological response. To get such a reaction from Raymond Massey in *East of Eden*, director Kazan had to literally shock him into it. Knowing Massey to be an extremely proper gentleman, the director arranged for co-star James Dean to utter a non-scripted torrent of obscenities at the crucial moment in a dialogue scene. Massey's utter shock might be deemed Oscar-worthy.

Though it is usually not paid much attention, I have found that actors playing at being asleep or awakening from sleep rarely seem truly convincing. There is a slackening of muscle tone in sleep that cannot really be acted.

Realizing that certain conditions are recognized by their physiological effects and because *condition and effect* are emotionally tied to each other, one can sometimes resort to what Carl Dreyer called "going the other way," or work from the effect inward.

I had an occasion to use what might be called physiological trickery in a scene I created in a film about the death-row celebrity Caryll Chessman. Chessman was on the row for 12 years before he was finally put to death in California's San Quentin prison gas chamber. During that time, he had seen more than 50 men march past his death-row cell to their executions. I decided to visualize this experience by depicting a parade—seen largely from an angle behind Chessman—of condemned men of all ages, colors, and sizes passing him on their way to their deaths and sharing a final hand shake.

Prior to deciding to make this sequence, I was allowed only fifteen minutes with Chessman in a small cell set up at San Quentin for visitors of death-row inmates. I only had time to grab a few quick shots. I filmed several of him standing at the bars of the cell looking out into the corridor and another shot, inside the cell, sitting down and reading. For the "parade of faces" sequence I was forced to improvise something in a minimum-security section of the Chino Institution for Men, using real prison inmates to play the doomed men and without Chessman present. I cast for a back-of-the-head look-alike from among the inmates to *play* Chessman filmed from behind. The pompadour hairstyle Chessman favored was popular in the prison, and I easily found a double. (When intercut with my real Chessman shots, there was no jar.) At the end of a parade of faces, I wanted to create a particularly telling moment by concentrating on a very young, very terrified prisoner. The young inmate I chose to play the part—who was, incidentally, due for release within a few weeks— was eager to do well for the camera, but had difficulty playing his doomed moment convincingly. I reasoned that his terror would have such outward signs as a constriction of the chest muscles and a resultant shortness of breath. I asked him to do as many rapid push-ups as he could manage and then rushed him into the scene. He had exhausted himself and, on camera, desperately reached out for air, producing long, poignant shudders, which the viewer readily accepted as the signs of his terror.

Politicians and Other
Amateur Actors

As mentioned earlier in this text, I was hired in 1976 to make a 15-minute film about Gerald Ford for screening at the televised Republican Party convention. It was not my first political film, so I was aware that working with politicians presents many special problems for the director—primarily in getting them to sound natural and spontaneous whenever they address the camera. Politicians often seem to have a readily available array of buttons waiting to be pushed, rather than the normal sensory means of communication. Behind every button is a politically correct cliché.

President Ford is an amiable and attractive man, but not a particularly animated one. I decided early in the taping of the piece that I would not use the device of direct interview, because Ford's responses to questions tended toward the mechanical and were delivered in a rather flat and uninteresting voice.

While at Camp David, preparing to film the presidential family at lunch, I had some free time on my hands. Someone mentioned that the President had some free time too and would be willing to be interviewed. I found myself somewhat unenthusiastically agreeing to do the interview, which did not go well from the very start. The President was leaden in his delivery and, despite my efforts to the contrary, his buttons were pushed and he delivered the typically canned-sounding snippets I wanted to avoid. I asked to take a break, during which I complained to the president's son, Jack, that I was unhappy with the results thus far.

He asked me to let him try asking questions. Since we intended the interviewer's voice to be eliminated in the editing, I quickly agreed.

Jack began, like a Berkeley radical, with questions that attacked his father's policies. Dad responded quickly. His blood rose, his features livened, and his comments in defense of his conservatism were sharp, cogent, and totally fresh. We were interrupted for lunch and I couldn't wait to resume the interview after eating.

Unfortunately, after lunch Jack had second thoughts about playing the radical goad and demurred. It also turned out that the earlier exchange had been so passionate that the voices had become inextricably mixed and required that Jack be identified if the interview were to be used. Though I thought it would have been wonderful to keep the interview and reveal how tolerant Gerry Ford could be of political divergence in his family, I also knew how politically naive any such hope was. The interview was not completed.

Politicians often rely on seemingly well-rehearsed responses to protect themselves from politically damaging statements. This protective wall of automatic responses, however, is obvious to many and makes what they say less credible.

A director has similar problems when trying to animate the performances of non-actors and barely trained amateurs who, for whatever reason, freeze or become visibly uncomfortable when the camera turns on. In the case of interviews, a subject may fear making himself vulnerable by revealing the true and imperfect self he normally is at pains to hide. Psychoanalyst Carl Jung labeled this defensive shell the "mask." If the director wants to penetrate the mask to the "real" person beyond, he will have to find his own version of Jack Ford.

The Non-Actor in a Drama

When non-actors play characters in a dramatic film, it is often best to keep them in non-speaking parts. An untrained voice is hard to hide. This is less of a problem when the non-actor is a performer in another field (music, dance, etc.). Such an individual is already conditioned to temporarily live within an internal world of the imagination and not be diverted by his immediate surroundings.

Awareness of the camera can overwhelm the non-actor, producing a wooden performance. It can cause him to reveal his self-consciousness by actions like quick darts of his eyes toward the director or camera lens or embarrassed smiles toward persons who may be observing him. Self-consciousness or consciousness of the camera is a failure to maintain concentration on the content of the scene. It transmits itself directly to an audience, whose attention then also wanes. To help remedy this problem, any task that demands total attention may be suggested to the actor as a way of diverting his mind from the camera and himself.

Vorkapich observed that the only actors without self-consciousness (and who, incidentally, also escaped becoming old-fashioned as to acting style), were the animals appearing in films. The performances of the German shepherd Rin Tin Tin in the early days of movies, or his successor, the collie Lassie in later films, were always consistent, always contemporary. I think acting has become better since Vorkapich's day and Lassie is no longer the only actor who hasn't gone out of date.

The attention-absorbing task can be simple and anything that doesn't conflict with the demands of the scene—driving a car, preferably with the more attention-demanding stick-shift, threading a needle, lifting weights, or solving an arithmetic problem in one's head. An audience interprets the actor's concentration as being relevant to his situation. A classic example of this was demonstrated by the early Russian director Lev Kuleshov. He showed how editorial juxtaposition, in effect, can create the acting. When a serious, bearded, well-dressed man is portrayed with his chin on his hand, as if in thought, and the next cut is to a child in bed, the man appears to be a doctor pondering the treatment for a sick child. When the exact same shot of the man is juxtaposed with an image of a slice of pie, the bearded man is merely hungry and thinking about food.

MEANING THROUGH JUXTAPOSITION
THE KUSHELOV EFFECT

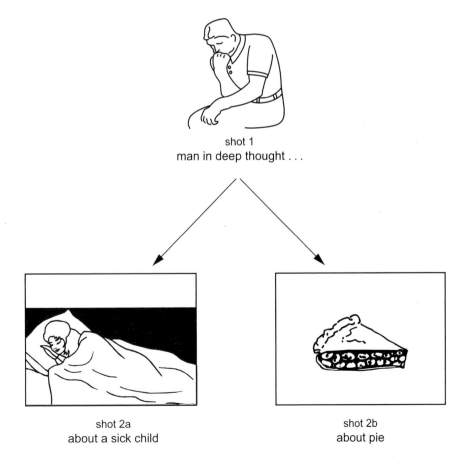

shot 1
man in deep thought . . .

shot 2a
about a sick child

shot 2b
about pie

Non-actors and some professionals can have difficulty with complex mood changes that occur on camera, such as gradually shifting from tears to laughter or from rage to calm to rage again. Rather than settling for a weak performance, I have sometimes sacrificed the advantage of seeing the mood changes happen on screen and used a different camera setup for each emotional peak, relying on the shots to be intercut.

An opinion I have often heard is that movies are a medium of reaction rather than action. I've never understood why this statement is uttered with the absolute "are," but I agree that reaction shots are useful in intensifying the focus on the action and suggesting to an audience how to react to whatever is presented to them. More than most of us would care to admit, the reactions of others affect our own judgement. Man is a social animal, conditioned (in order to forge a peaceful society) to respond as the pack does. The "reactors" on the screen lead us into our own responses in the audience. We may not be puppets, always imitating mass opinions, but we are all nudged in that direction.

I've always found humor in audience-reaction shots, particularly as portrayed in the older movies. I have imagined extras who exist exclusively to play part of an audience: distinguished looking mostly, with tuxedos and upscale gowns at the ready, practicing ways they can show indifference turn into enthusiasm; couples who rehearse turning toward one another with a smile and a nod to acknowledge that the star of the movie is achieving his or her big breakthrough in a performance.

When the non-actor must speak, it may be best to make that speech short and in reaction to someone else's statement or action. It also may help the player if he does not have to give an actual line from the script, but is able to find his own way of expressing the same idea. He must, of course, be aware of what ideas are expected of him. This technique of improvisation is sometimes used throughout an entire film striving for an exceptional realism.

Having the player listen to the director or a dialogue coach or even an experienced actor say the line first and then try to imitate it is probably a method of last resort. Such technique is frowned upon and even considered sacrilegious by many, but I have, at times, been forced to use this approach and have made it work adequately—particularly when the statement is reduced to as few words as possible, the player repeating them for the camera before he has had too much time to think about them.

An actor may wish to change lines he is not comfortable with. I tend to go with an actor's wish at such moments, but I must then pay serious attention to what he finally says. The writer has usually toiled hard to create and polish his dialogue. It can reflect more than a single level of meaning, and has often been carefully pruned for content, rhythms, and suitability to a character's time and place, things that may get lost with a change. But the actor knows what he has a hard time saying convincingly. "Ah," you may say to yourself as you part with some favored lines, "and they looked so good on paper!" Nonetheless, in this instance, it's best for you and the actor to find another way to say them. One must take care, however, that a small change does not have an unforeseen or undesired consequence in a story.

Director Irv Kershner, a student at USC in the Vorkapich era (and who was lured into films by Vorky), told me about an incident when he was directing Harrison Ford as Han Solo in *The Empire Strikes Back*. Just as the enemy is about to embed a captured Solo in concrete, Princess Leia, also a captive, tells him, as per script, that she loves him. His scripted line back to her was, "I love you, too." Kershner couldn't accept the idea that Solo, the story's cocky daredevil, would quite bring himself to say "I love you," no matter what his circumstance. So he changed Solo's line to "I know."

The simple "I know," uttered with a confidence that bordered on the cocky, makes quite a difference. Rather than a more conventional yielding to sentiment, Solo only acknowledges or accepts Leia's love for him. Both responses could be considered valid. Facing the immediate prospect of entombment, Solo might have reached a moment of enlightenment and acknowledged his deeper feelings or, being the man he had been playing with his irrepressible confidence and not inconsiderable ego, he might have only nudged over a wee bit and said, "I know." The small change, however, created a slight alteration in the arc of the Princess Leia/Han Solo relationship. Depending on Solo's answer, from that moment forward a love commitment either had been made or had still to reach a point of mutual acknowledgment.

The Trained Actor

An actor with formal training may be able to play Shakespeare, but may find it difficult to be without some degree of artifice on film. When possible, allowing the player to make up his own lines may help with this problem, but not every actor is comfortable with improvisation. Some very good actors find it frightening and need the security of a script. Obviously, the intent to improvise should be made clear to any actor considered for a part that will require it.

The veneer laid on by an actor's formal training—even with fine and subtle actors—was a concern of the distinguished French director Jean Renoir. He made a small film describing a technique called The Italian Method for erasing this gloss of artifice. It involved asking the actor to go through his lines with the director, who then calls attention to what he considers the slightest bit of actor excess. At these moments of artifice, Renoir had the actor repeat the line over and over until he got him, in Renoir's words, "to take the acting out of it." It was, the director said, like ironing a cloth to flatten out a wrinkle.

For the actor and the non-actor alike, self-consciousness must be overcome. Every time the actor's performance projects the mannerisms of his screen persona rather than the character he is supposed to play, the hot iron could be applied.

Often what must be ironed out is simply habituated style, which can be hard to isolate because it comes from the actor's proven and effective arsenal of the tried and true. And those actors who, relying on their habituated styles, deliver professional performances with a minimum of fuss and can work quickly are hired more frequently, particularly for the demanding tight schedules of television.

When directing, the question may become whether you will settle for what is good and works or whether you will risk going for more if you think that can be achieved, knowing, among other things, that doing so may pull the actor out of his familiar and comfortable acting mindset and make him nervous about possible failure. Note also that this effort will take time and, therefore, be measured by the money clock that ticks relentlessly. It is understandable why so many directors are inclined to accept what the actor delivers easily.

I directed a television hour called *Lincoln, Trial by Fire*. A fine actor, John Anderson, who bore a resemblance to Abraham Lincoln and had played that historic figure in a number of films, was cast to play him. John gave a strong performance: masculine, projecting a sense of feeling the weight of his office and the human costs of the Civil War. His voice was sonorous, his manner grave and dignified. I was convinced he had indeed given a very fine performance. When the show aired, I called John from a picture location to share what I expected would be his pleased response. It was the first time he had seen the show and I found him troubled. He surprised me when he said, "I'm disappointed. I failed to reach for it. It was all old hat!"

"What do you mean, John?" I asked. "Everyone here loved it. I loved it."

"No," he said, "that was the same old stuff—just the same old stuff."

Suddenly, I saw what he meant and I knew he was right and that I had failed him as a director, just as he had failed himself. What John had delivered was a deception. It was good, but it was just a repetition of roles he had already played a hundred times, utilizing sure-fire technique, but no original discovery. I believe John did have it in him to find a higher level of performance if I had encouraged him to *go for it*.

On the set, I had been seduced by John's performance. Of course, any competent acting is a form of seduction. John and I were friends; I wanted him to do well. Watching his live performance, I got all his vibes rather than seeing only the performance. After this experience, I decided that whenever possible I would watch the actor's performance on a video monitor, which creates a measure of objectivity through separation. Live, John was seducing me with his actor's instinct for playing to the audience—with skillfully pregnant pauses, a weighty delivery, and voice tricks—and I let him.

It is said that the American President can have no personal friends since he must make impartial decisions for the good of the nation at all times, no matter whom he may offend. The director need not be callous, but he must strive for that same impartiality for the good of his film. He has the same intention as the actor, to get the best possible performance, but the director's responsibility is to weigh the balance of the parts in support of the whole. If the actor seduces the director, the director also seduces himself. Only the performance matters. The director should always ask himself if the actor can do it better. If there's opportunity, he should say, "Let's give it another try."

Internal or External Perspective ▬▬▬

Moulin Rouge!, starring Nicole Kidman, makes highly imaginative use of imagery and film editing. It is something of a visual feast created by striking set design, a seamless use of miniatures, flamboyant costuming, fluid camera movement, and physical action. This film is instructive both where it succeeds and where it does not.

A subtle point not often raised is the difference between what might be called "internal" and "external" perspectives. With the filmic approach, concerned as it is with the play of graphic elements, there is a tendency to concentrate on external effects, which are good at creating such relatively crude forms of emotional or sensory responses as excitement, fear, exhilaration, agitation, and even delirium, but fail to lead us into the internal life of a film's characters. Without gaining this internal perspective—empathy—we in the audience are witnesses to, but not participants in, what we see.

An audience may experience only an external perspective simply because it is not engaged enough with the persons on the screen. They are strangers to us. As Harry Lime, a character played by Orson Welles in *The Third Man*, asks his one-time friend Holly Martins (Joseph Cotton) while looking down at people from their perch on a great Ferris wheel, "Would you really feel any pity if one of those dots stopped moving forever?"

The creation of empathy is a main value of the closeup. Closeups—particularly ones in which we look into both eyes of a character—lead us to intimacy. Visually, only the eyes can take us down this path. The parallel film within the audience's mind (Carl Dreyer's "third dimension of a film") accumulates via this intimacy. But not every closeup is effective. Some faces are inscrutable masks, some are alive with the process of living. Here is where the quality of the actor comes in.

I raise the rather weighty issue of generating empathy because, to my mind, the otherwise-brilliant *Moulin Rouge!* unfortunately falls short of generating much of that all-essential quality. At the film's beginning, we are treated to an inventive and exuberant introduction to the musical ambience of the Parisian demimonde at the turn of the last century by entering the café-theatre-dance-hall Moulin Rouge, made famous by the painter Toulouse-Lautrec. We are quickly introduced to its dancer, singer, courtesan, and star, Satine (Nicole Kidman), in an unusual and sexy performance. The sequence, full of visual pizzazz though it may be, goes on too long without offering an emotional connection to the Satine character. We are given an enormous diversity of camera angles. We are not starved for visual enrichment or the "three-dimensionality" (in the physical sense) of our environment, but we are impatient without a place, as it were, to hang our hats and, more importantly, our hearts. A story, whether told with words or pictures, needs to *begin to roll*. For events to be linked together, to appear to lead us someplace, the tension of expectation must be created.

A memorable actor can lure us into his state of being. How the great actor does this seems magical. Sometimes, even in a film without a discernable storyline, a great actor can grab us—we don't want him to leave the screen. He can reach our hearts with the story before we know why we are involved. Unfortunately, the way Ms. Kidman's beautifully formed and photographed facial features are used in *Moulin Rouge!*—a visual concentration on her cool beauty—tells us very little. She is not pushed to project more than a tepid, if not an emotionally cold, personality. Satine's story, an old and classic one of choosing between true love and survival, is predictable, yet it could have been engrossing nonetheless if the actress had brought her character to life.

Psychological Preparation for a Shoot ▬▬▬▬▬▬▬▬▬▬

Vorkapich once described a group of students he was accompanying to a film location as having spent the entire hour-long trip engaged in "kidding around." No one in the group thought to bring up the subject of the filming that lay directly ahead. Later, he lectured his classes on the importance of preparing seriously for their work. He described how classic Chinese artists never began to paint without a period of meditative preparation. They understood that entering the world of the imagination required a detachment from the normal world around them. They demanded from themselves an *ardent change* from the normal focus. The world of paint and canvas exists according to its own rules and requires the painter's total concentration. Vorkapich argued that the filmmaker must prepare himself for the screen with equal seriousness.

Moviemaking often requires long, tiring hours, sometimes under difficult physical circumstances and other stresses that might make concentration difficult. At times, I recognized that my work was weakened because I lost the intensity I had usually been able to maintain during filming. On long shootings days, it sometimes became uncomfortably clear that work at the end of the long day lagged in energy or invention. True, good filmmakers often have unusually high energy levels. However, it is perhaps obvious that getting sufficient rest is not to be neglected without risk.

Unlike writing or painting or composing, the financial costs of moviemaking create great pressure to get the filming right the first time. Before production, the filmmaker can utilize his time in polishing the script, visualizing his imagery and structure, perhaps using the aid of a storyboard, carefully casting (testing actors when possible), rehearsing without cameras, and engaging in any other form of research from which he can build within his mind the environment of place, time, and culture where his story occurs.

I enjoyed a unique and most favorable environment while making *The Surrender at Appomattox*. The majority of the extras we employed to represent soldiers and townspeople could in a unique way be said to live Civil War-period lives. They were members of social organizations whose purpose was to costume themselves in absolutely authentic clothes and uniforms of the era and to reenact major Civil War battles on ceremonial occasions. They fashioned authentic replicas of firearms and all manner of household and field implements—even the buttons on their shirts—and gathered together often to share Civil War lore. To these people, the Civil War and its main participants were as real and present as next-door neighbors. Assisted by these experts, the cast and I became steeped not only in the details of Civil War history, but in an all-embracing mid-19th-century atmosphere. In the film's final scene, when Michael Fairman, the actor playing Robert E. Lee (and who, when properly made up, bore a striking resemblance to the war-weary general) rode his horse to the Appomattox Courthouse to surrender, the actors playing the townspeople were heard to exclaim quite spontaneously and with apparent sincerity, "It's Bobby Lee, Bobby Lee himself." Later, sitting in the actual Maclain farmhouse where the surrender took place, Fairman recalled having an experience of disassociation from his own body, feeling that his image in the hallway mirror moved independently of his flesh-and-blood self.

I cannot explain the occurrence other than as an extreme example of the power of psychological immersion in a world of the imagination. One speaks of things like "being possessed." Isn't that the actor's function—to become possessed by the spirit of a person other than himself?

Fairman has gone on to a long and successful acting career, and the power of his performance and that of the other actors helped create a quality film that earned professional awards and critical praise.

Working Within Limitations ▬▬▬

The filmmaker has a great degree of malleability afforded to him in the editing process. As I discussed earlier, he should extend this malleability as far as possible by his direction—preparing for both the foreseeable and the unforeseeable.

Sometimes, special opportunities arise to make "pickups" after sequences have been edited, when the desired end result becomes apparent in a way it wasn't during regular production. Picking up a scene can be a very pleasant time for the filmmaker, who then has a rare moment of absolute certainty about his needs. It can, therefore, be a most efficient process. But the cost of making a film—the amount borrowed and the growing interest on the debt—makes quick completion desirable. An editor, therefore, nearly always begins work while a shoot is ongoing. But directors have a union-guaranteed right to a first cut and some directors of influence resist having any serious editing occur while they are unable to be present in the editing room.

Rarely during the history of moviemaking has a director had the liberty Charles Chaplin enjoyed when directing his silent classic *City Lights*. He spent two years in production, re-shooting and rewriting scenes. A year into the production, he changed his leading lady. Luckily, the film turned out to be marvelous, but even the powerful and immensely success-ful Chaplin never had similar freedom again.

To fashion work of quality and ensure his own professional survival, the director must make the most productive use of the time available to him. It is foolish for him to try to outwit the production executive minding the cash flow. A fundamental reality is that filmmaking is costly, and costs can easily get out of hand. If the money is gone, there is no way of making either a good film or a bad film.

Some readers of this book may be contemplating making a low-budget movie withdigital equipment. Despite the cost savings this technology allows, even digital movies still cost substantial money. The best way for the filmmaker to prepare for filmmaking's inevitable problems—financial or otherwise—is to be flexible. For example,be willing to substitute a new sequence that can fit the budget when what was planned cannot.

Choosing the Battle of the Wilderness as the battle to be represented in my Appomattox film led to a style that stressed the unseen. As mentioned earlier, I felt that the hidden enemy in the final cut might even be more effective than a more visible one had there been the budget to provide a battle on a grander visual scale.

The script for this film called for a scene on the night before General Lee's surrender, when General Grant, in his bedroom on the second floor of a farmhouse, suffers a migraine headache while his officers carouse and bang on an out-of-tune piano on the floor below. However, we could not afford to film the scene as proposed in the script. Instead, I chose to create the piano only as a thumping presence on the sound track and to visualize the carousing officers from outside merely as shadows on the downstairs window curtain. General Grant, we are told by the narration as the camera pans up to his dimly lit bedroom window, is suffering a throbbing migraine and sits on his bed, holding his fists to his temples. The camera outside moves slowly toward the small pane of the window's glass, the piano bangs away, mocking Grant's pulsing headache, and the wall around the window is dark, untouched by the dim light inside. At the brink of victory the mood is ironically solemn.

Less Is More

The "less is more" philosophy motivated Carl Dryer's planning of the crucifixion scene in a film he was preparing about Christ. All previous visualizations of that historic moment I have seen on film showed the nails being driven into Christ's palms, or about to be driven.

Dryer, however, planned filming from behind the cross, the impaling nails emerging through the back, splintering the wood—the force and brutality of the nailing made clear, but by indirection. The imagination is left to fill in the details, and a tasteful sense of aesthetic distance is maintained.

The horror genre is a place where the technique of indirection is nearly always used. In fact, the most frightening sequences are usually those in which the full horror is *implied* rather than seen. In 1942, producer Val Lewton, who specialized in B-movies, made *Cat People* on a relative shoestring. It established his reputation.

The lead actress in *Cat People* was Simone Simon. Her character had the discomforting tendency to transform into a deadly black panther when emotionally upset or aroused. Incidentally, the actual transformation is never shown: The panther is suddenly present and the actress is not, thereby maintaining a lingering uncertainty as to whether a transformation has really occurred—which suited the ambiguities of the story.

In one simple but effective sequence, Simone's woman friend who is in love with Simone's husband, and who also suspects the truth about her, prepares to go for a swim in a deserted gymnasium pool at night. The locker room is bleak, and she hears short, scuffling sounds. She grows afraid. The pool room is dark and full of menace. She flicks on the light. She hears an angry panther's growl reverberate against the tiled walls. She is terrified and dives into the pool. She treads water, looking around desperately. We wonder with her if a panther can swim. The panther sounds again, an angry snarl—louder, with even more reverberation. There is a fleeting shot of the panther's shadow. But where? We aren't sure. The terrified swimmer moves in one direction, then another—turning, turning. The next growl sounds as if it is on top of her. She gasps. At that moment, Simone Simon in human form, but wearing what seems a symbolic fur coat, emerges from some shadows. She smiles, offering the swimmer her hand to help her get out of the pool. She is natural, without hostility. The sense of terror is postponed, but as we know, not for long.

The scene's effectiveness was created with very economic means: an empty, starkly lit locker room and pool; the various panther sounds; the shadow of a panther on the wall; and, of course, only two actors.

Perhaps because we live in an age of slick special effects, contemporary movies too often make an effort to heighten the sensational by showing material that shocks, breaking the constraints of taste that have kept such material from being shown before. As each "shocker" is displayed, the next production is driven by audience expectations to come up with something even more violent or gross.

Early Westerns and gangster films were undoubtedly unrealistic when gun-shot victims fell to bullets that left no mark or blood. Contemporary gore movies have made me a little nostalgic for those simpler times. Perhaps those earlier films showed a classic restraint like the dramas of ancient Greece, in which all violence occurred off stage. Violence, like explicit sexuality, sends very strong signals to our most primitive responses and tends to overwhelm all other messages.

British art critic Roger Fry went so far as to criticize the sensuous ancient temple carvings of India as being too sexy to appreciate aesthetically. Ancient Indian temple carvings are much more than purely sensual. They were carved to celebrate what in their era was considered holy: a celebration of the rhythms of life, fluidity and beauty in the female form, the wresting of sensuous appeal out of rough hewn stone, the inherent dignity that is expressed in the beautiful organization of forms. While I agree that an aesthetic distance is required in appreciating the subtler values of an art, I feel Fry was a bit too alarmed by the carvings. Sensuous material and even violence on screen can be dealt with in ways that have a formal beauty or psychological depth. Artistry provides a layered texture that can put the sensuous and the violent in perspective.

In the great films of the past, we find truly powerful sequences that are often simple, where information is disclosed by indirection, where images also become symbols. Such a moment occurs in *All Quiet on the Western Front* when a German soldier, Paul (played by Lew Ayres),slowly reaches his hand out from his trench to pluck a butterfly that has alighted on the ground just ahead. A French sniper takes aim—fires. Paul's hand suddenly jerks back in spasm as he is shot and killed. Paul's hand is mankind's reaching out for beauty in a world nearly destroyed; the butterfly is not only beauty, but fragility and transience, symbols of almost unbearable poignancy. It is an effect more powerful than a total image of Paul's bloody death might be.

In the great German director G. W. Pabst's silent film *Pandora's Box*, the memorable beauty Louise Brooks plays Lulu, the sexually generous, irresistible creator of havoc in men's lives. Her own end comes at the hands of Jack the Ripper, played by Gustav Diesel, an actor who–contrary to one we might have expected to see cast—possesses an unobtrusive handsomeness, but also an aura of sadness. One feels that women would be drawn to him without fear. On the street, a Salvation Army girl is moved to give him a sprig of mistletoe, even though he has refused her request for a contribution. Later, without money herself, Lulu solicits him. He tells her he is penniless, but she invites him to her room anyway. On the way, he deliberately discards the knife he carries. She sits on his lap and caresses his cheek. In a tender scene, he holds the mistletoe over her head and they kiss. But as he clasps her to him, he sees a knife on a nearby table. He becomes emotionally wrought. His hand clasps the knife. Again the image of the hand is used to tell us more than we see. We know she has been stabbed when her hand, holding tightly to his shoulder, seems slowly to relax, then falls away to rest inertly by his side.

Sound and Music and the Movie

Unless we are deaf, our visual experiences are rarely if ever separated from sound: shimmering leaves and the sound of wind, the accident and the noise of the crash, our chest heaves and our breath sounds. The world is never silent: The house creaks, air whooshes through vents, birds chirp, clocks tick.

The silent film was wonderful in the way it stimulated the development of visual expression, but movement in the movie image was never completely natural without its sound accompaniment. The movie house pianist or organist was brought in to fill this aural void.

Music "moves." In other words, it expresses itself through a period of time. It readily accepts being joined with other forms that move, e.g., dance and film. One has simply to contemplate driving a car with the radio or CD on to recall an intensification in the pleasure of feeling the "flow."

Joining music to film brought a deeper psychological and emotional sense to the action on the screen. Musical content enriched the psychological and dramatic quality of filmic experience.

Vorkapich was drawn to the joining of music and film, as is evident in his filmic dances to Wagner's *Forest Murmurs* and to Mendelssohn's *Fingal's Cave* overture. But he also felt that music was an old and very sophisticated art, while motion pictures were still in the crude beginnings of a relatively new kind of expression. He felt that most movie images are a kind of unrefined ore, a mishmash of the significant and the insignificant, while music was distilled and purified to its essence. Perhaps the most suitable sounds to associate with film, he felt, might be those that are less "pure," like the experimental "music concrete," which processes and structures prerecorded sounds. The sounds of movie music concrete may resemble sound effects, but they often aim for the emotionally expressive qualities of lyrical music written for traditional orchestral instruments.

The Worlds of Film and Dreams

When I was fresh out of film school, I had the opportunity to work on the low-budget film *Five*, written and directed by Arch Oboler. Arch encouraged his crew of ex-students to participate in early critiques of the script. I recall arguing that a particular action by a character was lacking sufficient motivation. My objection was overruled and the film was shot as written. Somewhat to my surprise, the scene I had objected to strenuously was inoffensive. Oboler, on my admission of surprise, commented that, as in real life, when you see something happen, you accept that there has to be a reason for it and you fashion one in retrospect. If the tiger is charging you, it is perhaps important to know if the big cat is hungry or just playful, but the fact of the charge is more real than the motivation. Figure it out later, it's time to run! I am not arguing against motivation in the actions and events in drama, only calling attention to the way that, in general, whatever is seen tends to be accepted as happening for a reason.

To some extent, this may help explain why French director Alain Resnais's films *Last Year at Marienbad* and *Hiroshima mon Amour* seem to disregard logical structure, yet still manage to intrigue. One was led to believe in the presence of a hidden significance. The consummate actors' convincing belief in the validity of their seemingly illogical actions nudged the audience toward an acceptance of the film's reality. The viewer, if he had the patience, was pulled into a vigorous attempt to deduce the film's meaning. These unstructured, or perhaps I should say obliquely structured, films have a dream-like quality, and dreams have always intrigued us.

Some of the editorial techniques already mentioned, such as leaps in time or space (via cuts, dissolves, etc.), joining images seamlessly by connecting movements to one another, and the use of the closeup to effect a change of scene are accepted as normal movie experiences. A pattern of seemingly illogical events can progress smoothly if there is an aesthetic fit.

In both films and dreams, a series of images are spawned by some internal force, be it exerted by the filmmaker or by the dreamer's unconscious mind. The connections between the images in film are the logical cause-and-effect patterns of the world within the frame. In dreams, images are symbols connected by a logic hidden in the unconscious. In both film and dreams, however, because we "experience" the events, we tend to acknowledge them as having reality.

Painters Salvador Dali and Georgio de Chirico, among many others, were part of the surrealist art movement, which celebrated dreams and encouraged the creation of bizarre, dream-like paintings. The surrealists felt that this dream nature in their art reached directly to the unconscious minds of viewers without having to be filtered through an intellectual process.

The surrealists were also attracted to making films, perhaps the most famous example of which was *Un Chien Andalou* by Salvador Dali and Luis Buñuel. They reportedly said that they threw everything away that was understandable and kept only what wasn't. Buñuel continued his filmmaking and later hired Jean-Claude Carrière, a young Frenchman who was to become a well-known screenwriter, to work with him on the script to *The Discreet Charm of the Bourgeoisie*. Buñuel announced to his co-writer that they would both have "the right of veto." Either of them could decide if an idea was good enough to keep, the only stipulation being that the opinion had to be delivered within *30 seconds* after hearing the idea. Buñuel's rationale was to circumvent the cerebral mind and find a direct path to the unconscious.

The surrealist movement influenced many later films, such as *Last Year at Marienbad*, and expressions of the drug/rock music culture. Surrealist-style disdain for the logical is evident even in the names assumed by many rock groups—Jefferson Airplane, Pearl Jam, Pink Floyd, and The Foo Fighters to name a very few. And, as has been noted in sociological studies, certain members of the drug culture make a virtue out of not rationally explaining or justifying themselves. This cultural phenomenon may be attributed to many drug-induced experiences that—like dreams and surrealist art—seem meaningful without being logical.

Surrealist concepts become relevant to us when we contemplate non-linear film structure. Linear structure is shaped to proceed in a more or less straight (logical) line from a beginning premise to a conclusion. Each step in the linear structure is a preparation for the next, and so on. The non-linear structure promises no logical sequence and, if containing a logical premise, keeps such premise well-hidden. It operates mainly by capturing your interest in spite of a lack of intellectual clarity. Most importantly, it aims to provoke emotion in a mysterious way. It does not aim to be understood, even though it may cause many to attempt an understanding.

While at USC, Vorkapich taught his theories in a class called Filmic Expression. I was thrilled to lecture to this same class some 30 years later. I encouraged my students to practice with non-linear structure, feeling that this would encourage more supple ways of thinking about the possibilities contained within the film form. I was surprised at the difficulty some students felt venturing into this unfamiliar territory. These few felt that leaving what they perceived as a logical world was threatening. I, in turn, felt that hanging on too desperately to the security of the explicable world was inhibiting to creative growth. I urged my students, in this age of computers and electronic copying, to "borrow" from existing videos and re-edit them. (For strictly personal or classroom use this violates no copyright law.) I suggest this practice to any reader who wants to play at the sport of finding new and unexpected filmic combinations. It will require some investment in equipment, but technological advances are making what is necessary available for a reasonable cost.

A relatively simple assignment that I gave the class was to jumble linearly constructed films or shuffle them together with another film. One specific assignment was to mix a chess game we shot in class with free helpings from a reel of Vorkapich montages. The most common pattern among the students was to see the chess game as a war and intercut it with war scenes. Considering that chess was inspired by real warfare, it was perhaps an unavoidable result.

Filmic Humor

I was inspired to give my class an assignment to play with visual recombination, in part, by a film I had never forgotten that was shown in my own student days at USC. Someone in a prior semester had assembled the film as a lark, but I found it more engaging than any of the other student work. It also taught me much about editing. It was called *The Jolly Reel* and consisted of film pieces gleaned from the discard bin of student projects over a period of several semesters. Someone with an imaginative nature had discovered how fascinating things often happened when images that had never been intended to be joined are juxtaposed. Some bits suggested poetic metaphors, but mostly it was just great fun. Humor, after all, is created by such sudden shifts from the expected.

One of the first staples of slapstick comedy is the pratfall, which is funny just because a character on his way somewhere has no idea at all that he will instead end up on his backside. The more earnestly he tries to resume his course, the more he falls and the funnier it gets.

The "running gag" is another comic staple, and *The Jolly Reel* had a delightful one created entirely by filmic means. Imbedded mid-reel is a shot of three men straining to move a large rock (a shot presumably extracted from some film about a construction project). Periodically, *The Jolly Reel* cut back to this same shot. By the fourth or fifth time, the shot becomes a joke. With each cut back, we have been made more aware of the strenuousness of the men's efforts and, despite the fact that we have visited the scene so often, the rock has not moved an inch. (Obviously, it was the exact same shot.) It becomes funny because, when a film cuts to something, we expect something of value to be added—for the narrative to move forward. We automatically expected the men to have gotten somewhere with their rock after so much time spent straining mightily. Instead, they become ludicrous.

Director Andrew Marton told a USC class about an even odder example of a running gag, an unintentional one, he had seen in a French film. A great tragedy had occurred in a small village and seven people were dead. Pallbearers are seen carrying coffins toward the gravesite in a long single file. To stress the enormity of the tragedy, the filmmaker cut back and forth between villagers and coffins as each casket was carried around a certain corner. However, by the time the cut was made back to the fourth or fifth coffin coming around the corner, the film audience began to titter. By the seventh coffin, they were laughing out loud. It became so funny because each cut back would normally imply that there had been forward movement, but each coffin shot turned up virtually the same. Finally, the audience, being frustrated and watching the same thing with each cut, wants to scream, "Is there an end to this parade?!"

Humor is best when it seems inadvertent, something that happens despite any plans to the contrary by the subjects on the screen or the filmmaker. The television program *Funniest Home Videos* is rooted in such missteps. Or the great W.C. Fields wants to hit a golf ball with his club, but newspapers keep sticking to his shoes. He doesn't have any better luck playing pool. Laurel and Hardy want to build the house, not have it fall down around them.

All these examples exploit the quality of the accidental. Therefore, film technique should not be used to "punch up" or "underline." One doesn't cut to the feet just before a clown takes a pratfall—that would anticipate the joke and show the filmmaker's hand. If physical humor is to work, everyone must seem to be caught off guard, the filmmaker too. Being caught off guard is the very essence of humor. The audience is set up to be unprepared for a surprise. When the gunman attempting to rob miserly Jack Benny points his gun and says, "Your money or your life," we wait on Benny's answer. We wait and we wait some more— the famous Benny pause. Finally, the gunman, exasperated (like the audience), cries out, *"Well!?"* Even knowing how miserly Benny is, we are surprised by how far beyond reason he can go. He pleads, "I'm thinking! I'm thinking!"

The lead characters in the best comedies usually have serious intent, not comical. They are absurd. Absurdity is sadness become funny. In great comedy, the absurd one is also, in his way, indomitable. Stan Laurel never really allows the fact that he is a constant cause of Oliver Hardy's troubles to depress him. He has no sense at all that they are both absurd. When the wonderful Peter Sellers played Inspector Clouseau (in the *Pink Panther* movies), whatever he tried to accomplish would usually end in debacle. But Clouseau did not accept the idea that he was responsible for his mishaps. He dusts himself off as if what has happened is an annoyance perpetrated by someone other than himself and resumes the role of the indomitable Clouseau. He may drive others crazy, but, as he moves on toward his next disaster, he remains a picture of calm.

The Responsibilities of
the Filmmaker

Making a movie is not a mechanical recording process. It is a process of transformation from a script to a real-time event to an experience on the movie screen. Each stage in the process has its own set of rules. Each stage must be given its due.

Moviemaking can be a demanding process, physically and mentally. Many people must be managed, cost overruns must be prevented. Time schedules and reality are not always complaisant, and nothing—not actors, equipment, weather, the script—ever works exactly as planned. Luck always plays a part in the final outcome, but the best luck nearly always comes to the well-prepared.

Shooting days can be hard and long. The director must take care not to tire, which may weaken his concentration. Making a movie is like setting up a complex factory for a one-time-only product. No two movies provide exactly the same set of problems; each is uniquely difficult.

A large group of people assemble. The actors, many with their own personal problems and agendas, are fearful—their careers are on the line. Everyone (actors and crew) looks to one person—the director—who must instill them with confidence. They must be able to depend on him to make something happen out of virtually nothing—intentions typed on pages of a script made into a film shown on movie screens and television sets around the world, where it will be judged, perhaps praised, perhaps dismissed.

I don't mean to imply that these responsibilities add only an enormous burden to the director. If he has knowledge of his craft, if he has prepared himself well, analyzed his material, chosen his ensemble of associates with the greatest of care, the challenge is to be savored. Moviemaking is an act of creation in harmony with many other people. In this way it is a social act, and the director's artistic success includes leading others to make the best efforts of which they are capable. I have enjoyed seeing the way in which an entire cast and crew respond to a striving for excellence. When the aim is high, so is morale. Everyone seems to feel better, difficulties are met as challenges to prove oneself and not as unkind or unfair acts of fate. These are the times making a movie is a shared achievement of enormous satisfaction.

Collaboration and
Directorial Integrity

With very few exceptions, moviemaking is a collaborative art. The degree to which a director actively collaborates with his visual co-workers—his cinematographer and his editor—will vary. There is no hard and fast rule. The need for a clear visual and editorial sense on the director's part, however, is indisputable.

I enjoy sharing the reasons for my directorial choices with members of my crew, my actors, and my editor. A director should realize that his final authority is not in question when he listens. Only added enrichment of the film can result—the film which, incidentally, carries his credit.

In the early days of my career, I worked as an editor and sometimes found myself disappointed in a director's work. I was tempted in my exasperation to sulk and grumble inwardly, "If only I had been in charge!" What a useless exercise that was! I gave myself a talking to. "Only the film matters," I repeated to myself. I acknowledged that who was superior or inferior was irrelevant. Everyone (including myself) and, most particularly, the film would benefit if I directed all my energy to devising ways that would make what was shot work best. This realization released me from a bind of dissatisfaction and made life better for everyone on the project.

The consummate professional, like cinematographer Conrad Hall, absorbs the director's point of view and merges it with his own. He acknowledges, "There can only be one leader of the band." This doesn't mean that the director may not, at times, be confronted by extremely strong-willed actors, cinematographers, and editors who can be very persistent and even somewhat devious in attempting to get their ways. All manner of intimidations can be attempted—an important actor can become inflexible in his interpretation or try to go around you to higher-ups, both the cameraman and the editor can ignore or misunderstand or simply use the strength of their personalities to stonewall your directives. These are not usual occurrences, so the director must hold his ground and accept nothing less than what he considers the best possible result.

The director's real source of authority is his own clear knowledge of what he wants. How the director stands his ground will vary with the occasion. I have known directors who had fits when not getting their way. It's not my style, but it sometimes gets results, though it's usually accompanied by unpleasant side effects—animosity and reverse intimidation and a cutting off of channels of communication. I prefer a quiet standing of one's ground, while showing appreciation for suggestions and communicating that one has given them serious thought.

The time or two that I have allowed myself to abandon my convictions linger in my memory with a bitter aftertaste. I am painfully jarred every time I see one of my films that, in its final form, includes what I knew beforehand to be a mistake that is now irrevocably imbedded.

Where Is Film Today?

The photoplay is overwhelmingly dominant in contemporary movies. The unique qualities we have called filmic are assets used only to serve the drama. For the fraternity of critics, most film scholars, and even the most rabid cinéastes, there is little noted beyond the story and the acting. The filmic quality is often relegated to a lower status labeled "technical" and is not recognized as a vital and expressive force. Nor is it used often by the moviemaker to its full potential for expressiveness.

I have often pondered how Vorkapich might have made use of the vast range of technical improvements that now enable the moviemaker to bring virtually anything he can imagine to the screen convincingly.

As I mentioned earlier, the greatest use of filmic technique these days is in television commercials, music videos, and action films. The usual aim in these projects is to create an exciting, visceral response, though commercials also do, at times, reach for a poetic or lyrical effect. In these cases, the emotional range and level is, of course, limited by the marketing purpose.

In the feature film *Crouching Tiger, Hidden Dragon*, directed by Ang Lee, a truly lyrical filmic quality is achieved. It might be interesting to delve for a moment into Chinese culture as expressed in the film. This ancient culture accepts the concept of an all-pervasive energy in nature called *chi*, which is the basis for Chinese traditional healing and martial arts. These arts practice the control and direction of *chi* energy and can, in some instances, demonstrate visible and dramatic results that cannot be explained by Western science. Theatrical exhibition of martial gymnastics are a popular form of entertainment, and the Chinese actor is often adept at displaying this art. Some of the powers claimed for the *chi* warrior, however, can only be called magic, but film and dreams are places where magic can be made to happen and appear real.

In *Crouching Tiger*, Chinese martial arts are given an extremely expressive rendering. The warrior practitioners are both men and women who possess reflexes, energy, and speed that elicit extreme credulity in the viewer. They demonstrate a dancer/acrobat's graceful physical balance. They can run up walls and even fly for short periods. The artful directing of the film and its mastery of state-of-the-art film technology present these amazing capabilities with convincing realism. There are no visible mechanical assists. Running up walls and flying are undoubtedly accomplished with the aid of cables, but electronic post-production methods make such aids invisible. These "fantastic" moments are also preceded by vigorous, faster-than-the-eye action, which utilizes the previously discussed *linkage of motion* to make them appear as natural extensions. There is a consistent and furious intensity to the battle, one remarkable feat flowing into another. We believe we are seeing it happen, *we believe what we see.*

The action is also a dance, the movements choreographed in a rapid-fire series of attacks and defensive interceptions. The acrobatics are dazzling, changing from one fighting technique to another so smoothly the eye barely follows. Sound, too, is meshed with picture in creative ways—sounds are exclamation points used to emphasize sudden movements, they are not merely used in lockstep with action.

Toward the film's end is a slower-paced battle of stunning imagination and beautiful design. The two combatants leap up into treetops to continue their fight. There they are slowed by their precarious perches on bending tree limbs amid billowing leaves. Their movements, however, are balletic even while realistic. The weight of their bodies is shown to join with the wind in swaying the trees.

Lyrical beauty and visceral excitement are smoothly blended. What is different in this film from an equally technically advanced Hollywood product is its elegance and restraint. There is no need for the action film's fiery explosions, mayhem, or blood and gore. I can see in *Crouching Tiger, Hidden Dragon* the virtuosity available to film these days to present a real world as nimble and exotic as dreams.

Slavko Vorkapich: An Afterword

Those who attempt to chronicle historical sequence always find it convenient to suggest possibilities for cause and effect. Though I am convinced that Slavko Vorkapich's influence on film technique was considerable, evident mostly in the visually adventuresome television commercial as well as in action and fantasy sequences in motion picture features, I do not want to overstate the case. Vorkapich was part of the historical stream associated with the early Soviet film pioneers Sergei Eisenstein and Vsevolod Pudovkin. One might even suggest that the cinematic "stream" began with the even earlier discovery of multiple camera angles, the greater visual diversity leading inexorably to moments of montage-like visual intensity in numerous films.

In addition, of course, the cross-fertilization of techniques among all filmmakers is ongoing. Who learned what from whom is not always clear.

But where Slavko Vorkapich was unique was in the way that he used visual analysis and movement together. It was not simply in breaking down a visually complex action into simpler parts or constructing a complex movement pattern out of simpler visual pieces, but in the *rhythmic* manner in which these elements were joined. His work displays rhythm as a dancer does and, as in dance, there are crescendos and diminuendos, quickenings and slowings, a mounting toward emotional peaks or a declining into death-like stillness.

Sometimes, when teaching a class, if he had no example on film, Vorky would describe a motion sequence or a filmic event with a graceful pattern of hand movements. His descriptions were quite beautiful, and I not only enjoyed his little hand dances apart from what they were meant to describe, but absorbed a real sense of the rhythms he meant to convey.

Slavko Vorkapich: An Afterword

Unlike the commercial that sets as its highest purpose the selling of toothpaste or relief from gastric distress, or the action sequences that aim only for a high level of excitation, Vorkapich sought to reach higher ground of art with elegant complexity. His montages sought to provoke a vigorous physical kinesthesis along with an evocative symbolism. Vorkapich's concerns were always with artistry, and, just as he told us in class, his filmic principles can prepare the filmmaker for that kind of achievement.

Acknowledgments

I would like to acknowledge the assistance of film historian David Shepard, who has been active in preserving the works of Vorkapich and John Hoffman. I want to thank my dear friend and co-producer of *Flight Forms*, painter, sculptor, and cartographic innovator Tom Van Sant, for his permission to use stills from that film. Thanks, too, to other friends and colleagues who share my enthusiasm for and gratitude to Vorkapich, such as Professor Marko Babac in Belgrade, Yugoslavia, who suggested that we call ourselves "the spiritual sons of Slavko"—a sibling bond that includes Conrad Hall and Art Clokey (the creator of Gumby) among numerous others, and Arthur Swerdloff and Sid Lubow who, as fellow students, partnered with me in our early careers in establishing Montage Films, a company dedicated to the Vorkapich approach to moviemaking. My thanks to Ms. Sayaka Ito for her sketches and diagrams for the book. And much appreciation to my editor, Jim Fox, for his knowledge of film and intelligent questioning of my thought. Most of all my gratitude flows to my wife, Joann, closest ally and sternest critic, whose help was invaluable in making Vorkapich's cinematic grammar translate into verbal expression.

It would be unjust not to gratefully note the significance to my filmmaking knowledge from the early opportunities offered me by that extraordinary producer and master salesman David L. Wolper. From the sixties into the nineties, long before public television provided a platform for the documentary, Wolper gathered many a struggling documentarian under his banner and provided economic viability, challenging opportunities, plus individual freedom to experiment and grow professionally.

Acknowledgements

Stressing the need to develop filmic sensibilities, Slavko Vorkapich resisted the idea of writing a book about his film principles. He concentrated his efforts, instead, on seeking to get the financing for what he called "a film about film." His death cut short that effort. But he did pen numerous articles that, together with the lectures he gave in Yugoslavia, were edited into a book by Marko Babac and published there. Entitled *On True Cinema*, the volume contains alternating pages in both English and Serbo-Croatian. It is available from Professor Babac, who can be contacted via e-mail at MBABAC@EUnet.yu.

In my decision to write a book exploring many of the thoughts of my old teacher and friend, I wrestled some with the concern that, in writing rather than fashioning a film on the same subject, I was, perhaps, violating some of the teaching I meant to honor. As I thought the idea through, however, I remembered the innumerable hours spent in discussion with Slavko and the insights I gained about film as well as a whole range of areas in psychology, the arts, and the joys of teaching. I decided that nothing would be lost and much might be gained from writing this book.